Fishing
Collectibles

RUSSELL E. LEWIS

©2005 Russell E. Lewis
Published by

kp books

An Imprint of F+W Publications

700 East State Street • Iola, WI 54990-0001
715-445-2214 • 888-457-2873

Our toll-free number to place an order or obtain
a free catalog is (800) 258-0929.

Library of Congress Catalog Number: 2004113679

ISBN: 0-87349-943-3

Designed by Elizabeth Krogwold
Edited by Dennis Thornton

Printed in China

Dedication and Acknowledgments

I dedicate all of my work to my wife Wendy. She is wonderful, and what more can one man hope for in life?

I also want to acknowledge the special help and encouragement given on this project to my acquisitions editor at KP Books, Paul Kennedy. The idea grew out of a conversation about the late Carl F. Luckey's masterpiece, *Old Fishing Lures*, and the need for more detailed photos and color to explain rod and reel collecting better. It is because he had the wisdom to encourage this work that it finally was completed.

I also want to thank my editor, Dennis Thornton of KP Books, for all of his hard work on many of my books on fishing and other collectibles that he has so ably edited. His design concepts and editorial ability make it a joy to write. It is so wonderful to send off a manuscript and then see it evolve into the final product with very little guidance from me once it is shipped to Dennis.

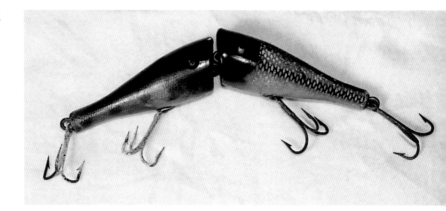

Creek Chub Plunkers

are some of the lures that started it all for me. My neighbor gave me three Creek Chub Plunkers when I was a young child and these two were saved from the ravages of being fished too heavily. The third one is a smaller size that has been repainted a number of times. These are perch on the left and the rare white scale color on the right. These are priceless to me.

$30-$100+ mint

Without my good friends Tony Zazweta and Ron Kommer, the book would be missing many items. Tony has found me some of the best fishing items in America to purchase. He has also brokered some great collections, part of which came my way. Ron has sold me his entire collection and also provided much information about companies or products, given his expertise and past writing experience about fishing. I also wish to thank Terry McBurney for his generous contribution of minnow bucket photos and information, and his willingness to share it with all collectors.

If any of you wish to contact me, I may be reached at ***findingo@netonecom.net*** or ***lewisr@ferris.edu*** at any time. For those preferring the mail, please drop me a line at Dr. Russell E. Lewis, Bishop Hall 515, Ferris State University, Big Rapids, MI 49307. Secure voice messages may be left anytime at (231) 591-3581. I respond to all serious inquiries in due time and I am always interested in data for future books and articles. I also buy and appraise tackle of all sorts, including rods, reels, lures, decoys, miscellaneous items as in this book, duck decoys and game calls. Any corrections should be addressed to me and they will be included in updated volumes.

Family keepsake

of my wife's from Beaver Island, Mich. This is a sentiment I am sure most angling collectors share.

$20+

Contents

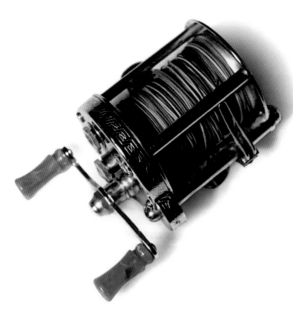

Pflueger baitcaster

is the first I ever purchased, an Akron from circa 1967-68 with the original line. The foot says "B" on it. I grew up using South Bend reels and a Pflueger Supreme, but could not afford to buy one as a child. I really wanted an Ambassadeur 5000 in the presentation box, but could not afford that either. This middle of the road baitcaster was good enough for a young man of moderate means, as it was a great functional reel and "new" to me. This is not for sale, but similar reels sell for $25-$50, depending on model and condition. See details in Chapter Two of many Pflueger reels.

$25-$50

Introduction

I am keeping this introduction short and simple, as my concepts on collecting fishing tackle should be well known by now, given this is my ninth book on the subject. My techniques for dating, preserving and collecting are explained in *Classic Fishing Lures,* also by this publisher, and need not be repeated here.

But a brief foreword is needed to thank the many other authors that have gone before writing about reels, rods and related collectibles. Their names are scattered throughout the book as well as references to their major books so there is no need to repeat them here. I am not the "pioneer," but hopefully my detailed photos and addition of many new fields of collecting make this a pioneering work in tackle collecting. This is my hope: that this becomes the "Luckey" reference book of rods, reels and miscellaneous tackle collecting.

A word about pricing is in order. I have used many actual sales prices in the text. I have also relied upon other data collected over the years in making judgments. If a general range given it is for an item in **EXCELLENT CONDITION.** Condition is discussed again in each section, but this must be kept in mind. Sometimes the item being shown is not in excellent condition, but the value given is for excellent condition unless I have stated otherwise.

Weber Tynex Spinning Line display stand

from Weber archives that I own. This nice stand is covered with some of my favorite "modern" lures: Punkinseeds, Fin-Dingos, Flutter Fins and Optics. Also shown are a prototypical Shakespeare and an old Weber streamer. Values: $200 for stand; lures vary from lower end Optics at $20-$40 to Fin-Dingos and Punkinseeds at more than $100 each.

$20-$100+ each

Chapter One:
COLLECTIBLE RODS

Fishing rods have become collectible over the past 10 years, with interest in them growing annually. Collectors have long admired bamboo rods. They bring hundreds to even thousands of dollars each, depending of course on condition, maker, age, rarity and the other factors determining the value of any collectible. There are many fine texts dealing with bamboo rods and that will not be the primary focus here. The coverage will include some bamboo, steel, pack and fiberglass rods. One of the most rapidly growing areas of interest in tackle collecting is in the field of collecting glass rods from the 1940s and 1950s. Many of these rods are shown. Photos of rods are shown detailing the wrapping styles, handle designs and other items that determine both age and value of rods. Some of the original cases are also shown, along with literature distributed by the rod companies.

Rods are very difficult to illustrate in their entirety. I have done my best to show close-ups of the details instead of concentrating on photos of the entire rod. Remember that rods are also given a special nomenclature regarding tips and blanks. A rod with three sections and two tips (one spare or one for wet and one for dry flies) would be shown as a 3/2. Details that become important to collectors are primarily in the following areas:

1. **Wrappings.** Collectors do not want rods that have been re-wrapped, as a general rule. Sometimes one finds one guide re-wrapped and this alone will diminish the value of the rod. A rod with all new wraps is not generally desired by collectors.

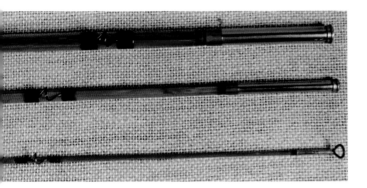

2. **Guides.** Along with re-wrapped guides, replaced guides greatly decrease the value of a rod. Of course, replaced tips are the most common ailment of a fine rod and will decrease its value. In bamboo rods, broken tips are even more common and will hurt the resale of a rod. If the bamboo rod is a rod that originally came with two tips, the presence of at least one perfect tip is nearly mandatory for most collectors. The absence of two perfect tips will decrease the value greatly.

3. **Ferrules.** The items that hold rod blanks together are called ferrules and consist of female and male versions. These ferrules must be original and the rod blanks must fit easily into one another. The best fit creates a small "pop" when one withdraws the male ferrule from the female ferrule on a metal-ferruled rod. Any rust, bending of the metal or replacement of ferrules diminishes the rod's value.

4. **Markings.** The original markings on the rod need to be clear, crisp and clean for a rod to maintain its highest collector value. Many rods were signed and numbered by their makers (bamboo and some high-end fiberglass), and most commercial rods were labeled with decals. A torn or worn decal or a stamping on the rod blank that is worn will decrease the rod's value. Mint labels will increase the value.

5. **Handles.** Rod handles are comprised of a number of significant parts, all of which have an impact on rod value. On the butt end, one may find a cap or protector that needs to be in place and unharmed. The reel seat needs to be intact and not marred. Any markings on the reel seat or the handle need to be crisp and clean. If the handle is wood or cork, it must be in fine condition without mouse gnawing or other damage inflicted by the angler, such as hook scarring. Sometimes the cork has been over-varnished and this will take away from the originality of the item. The reel seat must be in perfect functional condition, as well, for the rod to maintain its highest value.

include this "Manistee River Rod," shown in detail in Chapter One, made by Orie Wells and Jim Crawford of Traverse City, Mich., in 1979. According to Bob Summers, "It has an Orvis reel seat and I think the ferrules are also Orvis. Orie Wells and Jim Crawford were both local guys around Traverse City. Jim passed away about 10 years ago."

$355+

6. **Blanks.** All fishing rods are comprised of "blanks" (the rod itself) upon which the above are built. Blanks must be original and original length to be of greatest value. The shortening of blanks is a common problem with bamboo rods that the average collector fails to note. Any shortening of the blanks will take away from the originality of the rod. Normally, all rod blanks are the same length on the older bamboo rods, and many steel and glass rods as well. So if one simply checks this while examining a rod to purchase, it is a quick test to see if the rod is the original length. Also, the blanks need to be in good condition without major chips, dings, dents or scars.

7. **General Condition.** This would include whether or not a bamboo rod has been re-varnished, over-varnished (too much varnish when re-varnished), has a "set" in the rod tip (bent tip), any "setting" in the blanks (bent blanks), if the wrappings were the correct color if re-wrapped, and a myriad of other little things. The same issues can apply to steel or glass rods and will determine the value, along with age and rarity. Finally, rods were often packaged in "socks" that should be original and in fine condition (no holes, snags, tears, rot, etc.). The sock was inside a tube that also needs to be in good shape. Tubes were metal, hard cardboard or even bamboo in some instances. A marked tube correct for the rod is more valuable than an unmarked tube. However, collectors should keep in mind that any new tube costs $25 or more to protect the rod so any tube should be valued.

8. **Age/Maker.** The age of a rod is not nearly as important as its maker for the most part, especially high-end bamboo or glass rods. However, some of the first metal rods are more valuable than the later varieties if in clean condition with company markings. For the most part, I would concentrate on the maker more than age in determining rod values.

Rods and reels pose photographic challenges due to size, details, shadowing and glare problems. I have attempted to show enough details, and close-ups, to allow the average collector to easily identify an item. Also, values are included for each entry. As with lures, condition, condition, condition is important! The older or more rare an item, the less important is the condition. But it is still important to determine value. Values given are for examples in excellent to mint condition unless the actual value of a particular item is known from a recent sale or purchase, and then that value will be given.

Not as many folks collect rods as lures and reels. However, many are interested in adding at least a few rods to their vintage lure collections. Rods shown in this chapter should help identify some of the many different types available. I have taken photographs of rods by showing close-ups of the grips (handles), ferrules and wrapping, any markings on the lower rod shaft and an overview shot of the rod. The overviews really do not show much because of the length of a rod, but I thought it necessary anyway. The best way to tell rods apart is by examining the grips, ferrule wrapping and brand data or names on the shafts. Bamboo rod experts are also able to easily tell makers by examining the wraps and/or ferrules. Also, reel seats often identify a rod maker even without other markings.

Collectible rods include both bamboo and fiberglass. There are even some metal rods of interest to collectors. But as a general rule, bamboo and fiberglass rods bring more money and have a greater collector following. The early Gep, Richardson, Union Hardware, Bristol and Action Rods are just a few examples of collectible metal rods. Early Shakespeare, Tru-Temper and Philipson fiberglass rods are all excellent additions to any collection. Bamboo rods are a specialty in collecting and I would advise the buyer to beware, *Caveat Emptor*, in any dealings with others when buying bamboo rods. The value of a bamboo rod is rapidly diminished if it has been altered in any way, over-varnished, re-varnished, re-wrapped, or it has had broken tips replaced with others. I would suggest reading all of the many books available on bamboo rods prior to spending any significant funds on an addition to one's collection of a fine bamboo rod. Of course, if you are lucky enough to find any Heddon bamboo rod or Shakespeare bamboo rod in the field for a few dollars, buy it! But be careful before spending hundreds of dollars on a bamboo addition.

Rods shown and valued in this chapter are first shown in an introduction based upon valuation of known recent sales or other solid data based upon the author's selling and buying experience and research. Then rod maker or name of rod shows the remaining rods in alphabetical order. If neither the rod name nor maker is known, the rod will be in my final section in this chapter on unknowns. I have bought and sold hundreds of rods in all categories over the past 10 years and the valuation is based upon this experience. The fishing collectible market has been quite volatile the past few months and rods have been no exception to this rule, with prices widely fluctuating and in general being a

bit depressed. However, the better rods still command a premium and will have a following of hundreds of potential buyers for a good rod such as a Heddon Expert. A recent online auction had nearly 200 lookers. But beginning collectors need to realize that the rod market is much more specialized, and to a degree limited, compared to the market for reels, lures and miscellaneous items.

One reason for less demand for rods is lack of information about them. I hope this book will at least partly remedy that problem. However, storage and display are a real challenge with rods, as they should be stored vertically. That limits rod length to 7 1/2 feet for most of our modern homes. I have a nice old farm home with nearly 10-foot ceilings, allowing vertical display of longer rods; however, most cannot display an 8-foot rod properly. If one does not store a rod vertically it might set, especially bamboo rods. I have examined dozens of fine old bamboo rods found in the rafters of a ceiling or the floor joists of a home, only to determine set to the tip or mid-section due to being stored flat. Finally, please remember that rods were meant to be used, and one should not be afraid to enjoy the beauty of an old rod from time to time. I doubt I would fish with a $1,000-plus Leonard or Payne, but some do. However, I personally enjoy many of my glass rods. I actually use a variety of them each summer to test the differences and "feel" the evolution of our glass rod history. One of my favorites is an original Tru-Temper Uni-Spin, later made by Johnson. It is fun to still catch a bass or panfish on a rod built more than 50 years ago and realize that collecting has both form and functional aspects. Actually, this is one reason 7-foot bamboo rods bring more money in Michigan. One can still use them in the brushy stream sides common in pursuit of our brook trout. They also are able to be properly stored, adding to collector interest. Of course, out West the 9-foot and even 10-foot rods are often used on the big waters of western rivers. So the longer rods are appropriately valued more in that region. Regardless of one's reason for collecting old rods, I hope the following assists all collectors in their goals.

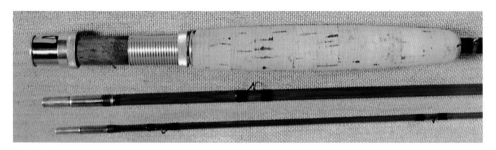

Rod Sales

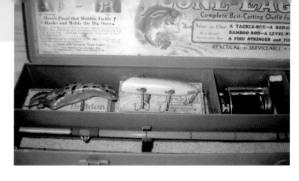

Heddon Lone-Eagle kit

This kit was recently purchased by a friend. It included a Heddon Lone Eagle bamboo casting rod, Heddon Lone Eagle reel, a Heddon Pal-On line spool, three "choice" Heddon baits in boxes (two were older downward bass boxes) and a Heddon stringer. One simply does not find an item like this very often and it came from a very "high-end" collection.

$1,000-$1,200

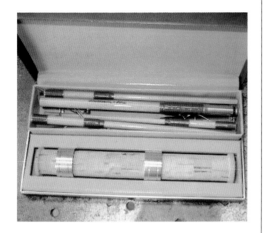

Abercrombie & Fitch Passport rod

in a leather case and an A&F fly box. This is my favorite of all fiberglass rods from the 1950s-60s. An A&F Passport rod breaks down into many small sections for travel. I have only seen two of them, this one and my own, in the past 10 years, so I know they are scarce.

$500+

Heddon Expert bamboo rod

in sock and tube. This is a Model #125, 8 1/2' 3/2 rod in F-HCH-D weight made by Heddon in original sock/ tube; condition is excellent. Value based upon sales online of two identical rods.

$400+

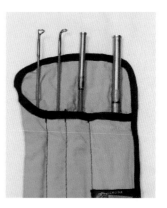

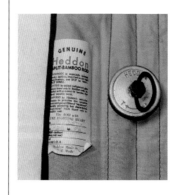

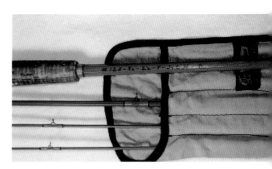

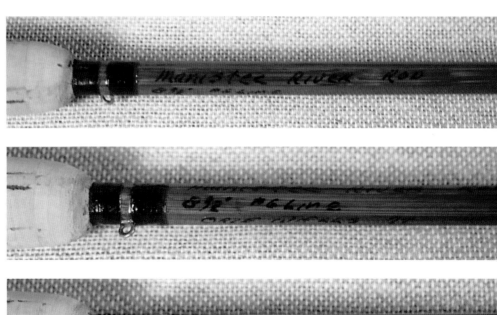

Orvis bamboo kit rod

#6 weight, 8 1/2' 3/1 rod, called the Manistee River Rod and made in 1979 by a rod maker in Travis City, Mich. This rod was originally claimed to be a Bob Summers rod when I purchased it from a dealer, but it is not. However, it is a very fine rod, showing great care in craftsmanship. The tip is slightly set. The rod is in very good plus condition overall and has extremely tight and beautiful "popping" ferrules.

$355

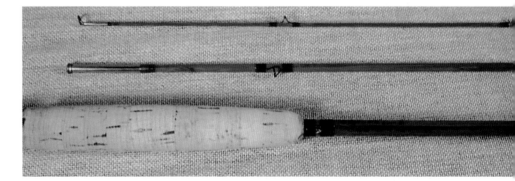

Four Fenwick examples

Fenwick Feralite glass rod, Model FF 807, 8' two-piece rod, 3 3/4 ounce for AFTMA #7 line; Fenwick Feralite FF 755, 7 1/2' two-piece rod, 2 1/2 ounce, AFTMA #5 line; Fenwick Feralite FL-90, Special; and, a Fenwick Woodstream (after Woodstream purchased Fenwick) with a custom wrap and a foam handle (details shown of the FF 755, FL-90 center section and the Woodstream model). Many rod makers and designers later copied the fiberglass ferrules. Fenwick glass fly and spinning rods sell for $75-$125 in most cases. These were valued at $70 each when all four were purchased together from another collector, but I was buying them for resale.

$75-$125 each

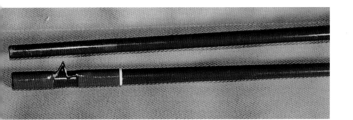

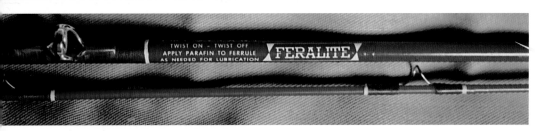

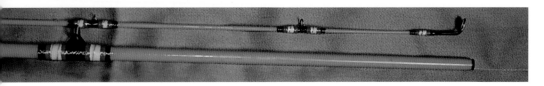

Montague Sunbeam bamboo rod

in correct sock, 8 1/2' 3/2 rod, fairly common for bamboo. Montague is on the lower end of bamboo collecting for the most part. Condition is very important on these rods, due to the plentiful nature of them compared to Heddon and other makers.

$250-$300

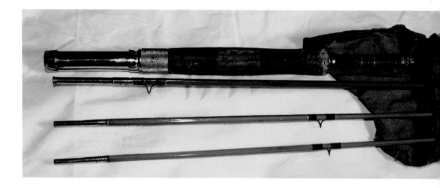

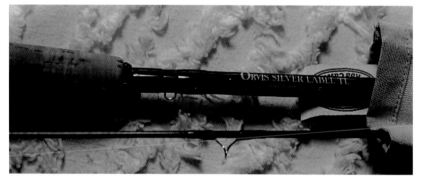

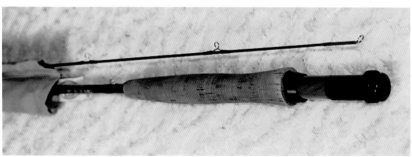

Orvis Silver Label Graphite rod

TL Mid-Flex 6.5, 9', #5 weight, excellent in a green Orvis carrying case/tube combination.

$85-$150

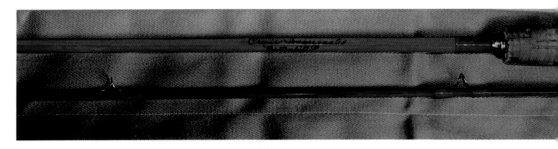

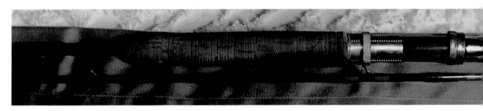

Orvis Battenkill bamboo rod

two-piece, 7 1/2', 3 1/8 ounce, HDY 6 line, Serial Number 77059, Impregnated Battenkill.

$425-$500

Ward's Thorobred bamboo rod

with correct sock and case. This nice 3/2 bamboo rod in 9 1/4' length was made by Heddon for Ward's. It is unusual not in its rarity as much as being original. Often the cases and socks are gone for these rods.

$350+

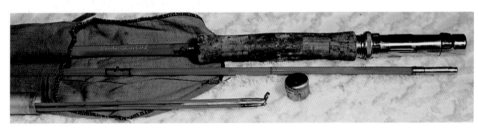

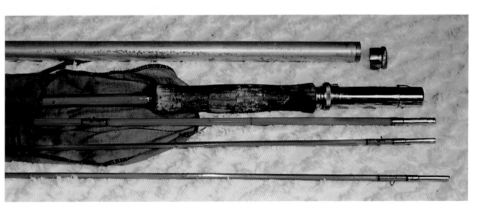

Two Heddon Pal Spook examples

Although neither of these are in pristine condition, rods in very good to excellent condition bring $65-$100 each. An excellent example with its original tube and bag is shown later in this chapter under Heddon that would command even more, likely $200+.

$65-$100 each

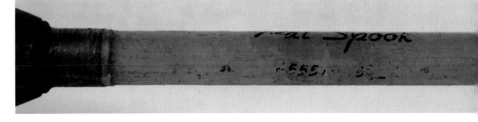

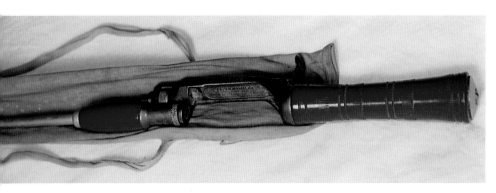

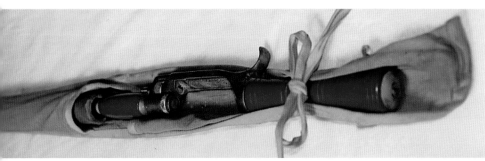

Action Rod Model 47

"Solid Steel with Bamboo Feel." The metal Action Rods by Orchard Industries were great rods and set the stage for the company's manufacturing of fine glass rods. I purchased this example in a private sale. Some of the rods are selling for more than $200, if pristine such as this one. Collector following of Action Rods is rapidly increasing. Sears and other stores, as seen later in this chapter, also marketed the rods.

$150+

Bamboo Rods

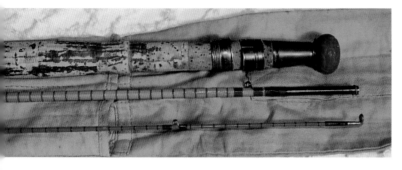

Allcock antique rod

is gorgeous and complete. It is a 3/2, with the tips being presented in a beautiful bamboo tube. The rod is from Redditch, England. One finds these tubes with a number of early bamboo rods and they add value to the find. This rod actually was found in a large tackle chest that held two fly reels and three bamboo rods, this one and two other rods that have since sold. Also shown is a related collectible by Allcock, a beautiful little Japanned tackle box with original Devons and other Allcock wooden lures and a fly wallet.

Rod, $500+; Box, $100+

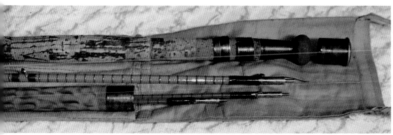

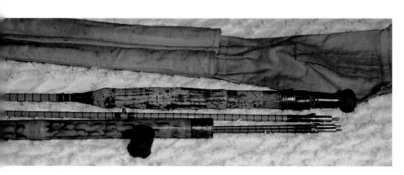

Airex Light spinning rod

in original sock and tube, early 1950s. Airex was the first big name in spinning in America. It sold both rods and reels, all of which are now collectible. This rod is pristine and came from an estate in Missouri along with a Langley and some other unusual rods from the early 1950s.

$75+

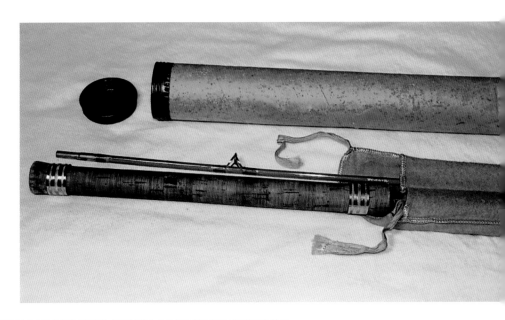

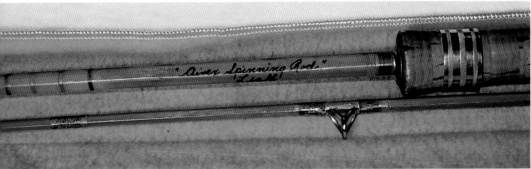

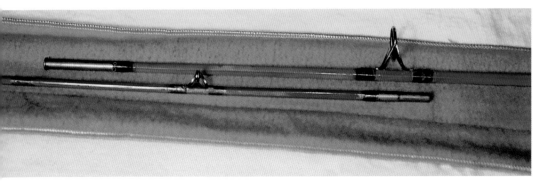

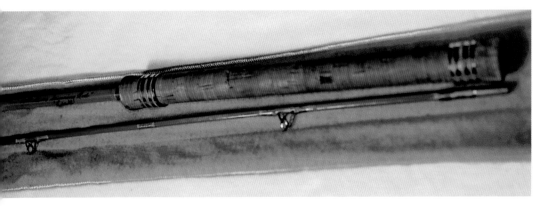

Two Granger Champion

3/2 bamboo rods. The first one is excellent and original and the second one shows examples of a broken tip, re-wrapped guides and varnish problems. The Goodwin Granger rods sell very well and have a high collector following. Some models will bring four figures.

$350+ if excellent; $100+ with faults

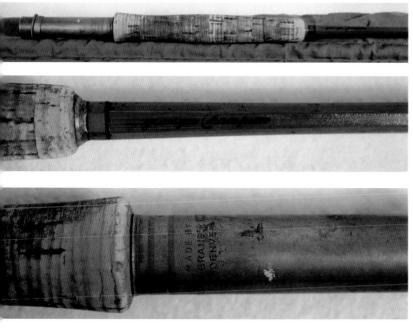

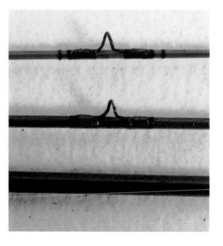

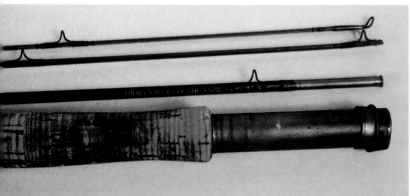

James Heddon's baitcasting rod

A few years ago, these sold for $25 or so, if pristine, as there was little demand for rods. This one is well used and would bring at least that much today.

$100+ if excellent

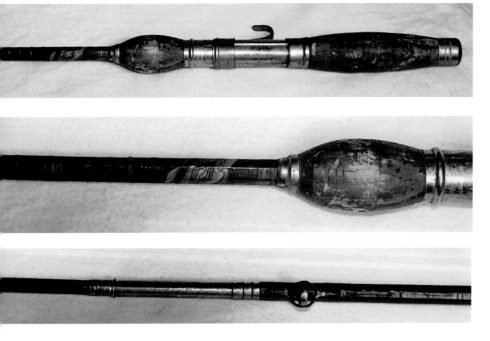

Horrocks-Ibbotson baitcasting rod

in decent shape. Note the different shape in the handles of this and the Heddon rod, and also compare the ferrules.

$75+

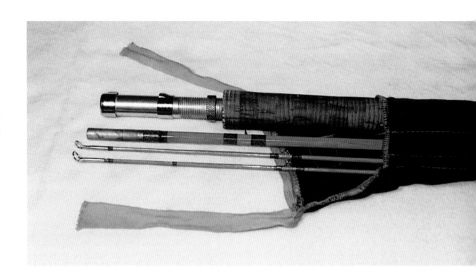

Herter's 3/2 fly rod

in original sock, in excellent condition, and a two-piece cardboard box for Herter's Cuxhaven fly line. The rod is valued at $150 or likely higher, as Herter's items are very collectible and in demand by both tackle collectors and Herter's collectors.

Rod, $150+; fly line box, $10

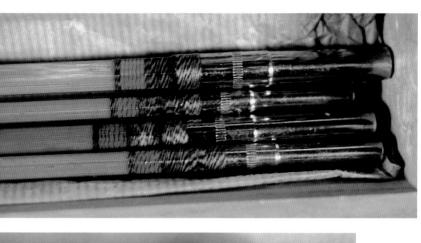

Japanese Prince bamboo rod kit

featuring a handle that works for spinning or fly fishing and a heavier blank for spinning, as well. These kits were brought to America by the thousands by returning Korean War veterans and were also imported during the 1950s through the early 1960s. This one is in nice shape, but Ron Kommer refurbished it before I bought it from him.

$75-$200 depending on quality

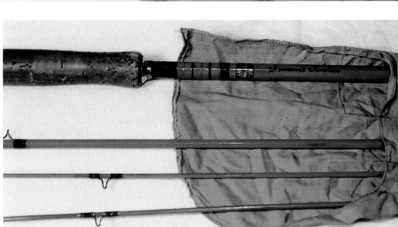

Montague
Sunbeam 3/2

*in its correct sock in excellent plus
condition. Also has its original tube.*

$250-$300

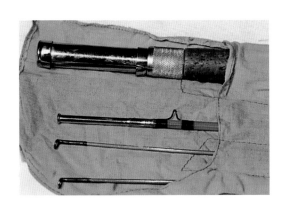

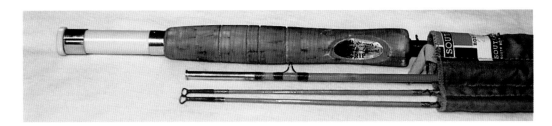

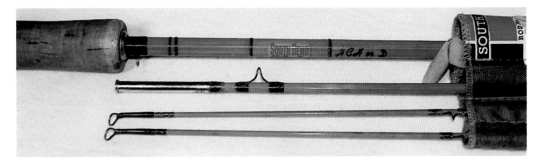

South Bend Model 24

*in correct sock, 3/2, 8 1/2', near mint, line
HCH or D, with Comfort Grip handle (area
indented for thumb while casting).*

$250-$300

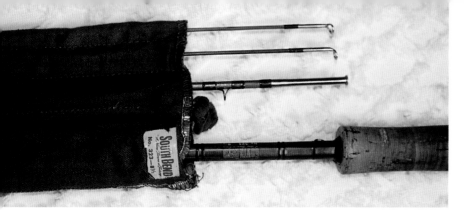

South Bend Model 323

in correct sock, 3/2, 8 1/2', near mint, line C or GBG, rod also marked William Murray above line weight markings.

$250-$300

Unknown antique bamboo rod

with one tip missing, 3/2, no markings.

$25-$50

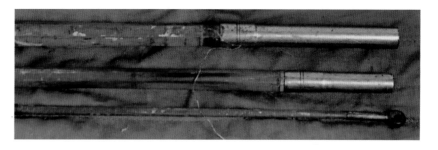

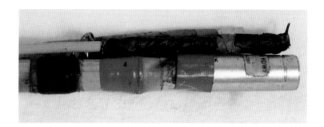

Unknown old-fashioned bamboo (cane) pole

that screws together. Note how the angler added line guides for casting. This was an antique store find for $25 that was worth it just for the Pflueger (Portage) Atlas model raised pillar reel.

Rod, $10; reel $25+

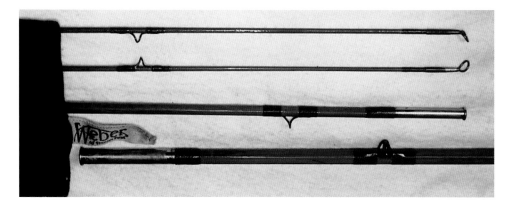

Weber bamboo fly rod

in correct tube and sock, 3/2. Weber had rods made for the company by Heddon, Shakespeare, Montague and other major rod makers. This is one of its top-end rods in near mint condition.

$500+

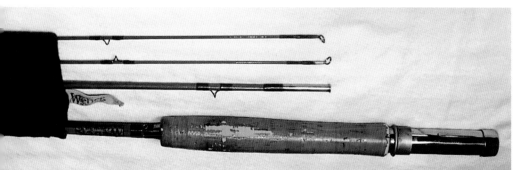

Wolverine trade name on rod

made by South Bend, 3/2, in correct sock and hard fiber tube. Rod is in mint condition.

$250-$300

Glass Rods

Four collectible glass fly rods

from the 1960s era. Right to left and top to bottom are an Actionglas from Orchard Industries, Eagle Claw from Wright & McGill, South Bend and a Cortland. Rods are shown completely under their companies later.

$50 minimum each

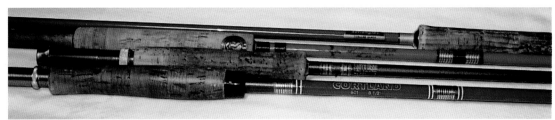

Airex two-piece spinning rod

This simple sliding ring reel seat was typical of many of the early spinning rods and was a design surviving into the 1970s on many rods. Airex was a major early contributor to spinning in America.

$25+

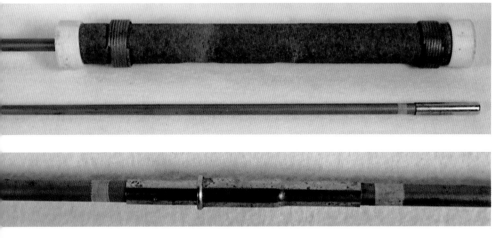

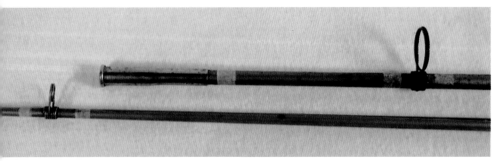

Berkley Fibre-Flex F-30 spinning rod

with the heart-shaped logo, 7'. Note the Fenwick type ferrules.

$35+

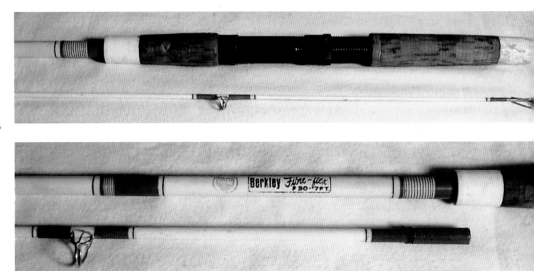

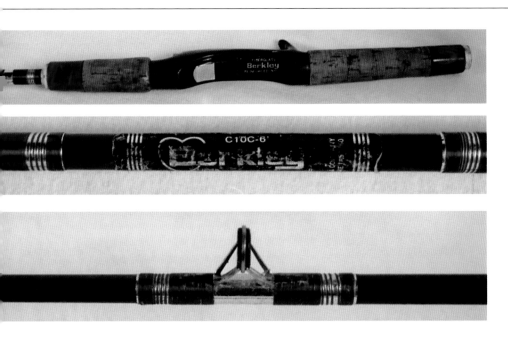

Berkley "Cherrywood" C10C casting rod

made in Taiwan, 6'. Berkley made the Cherrywood line to compete with Shakespeare's line of Ugly Stick rods and they were very fine glass rods. I have fished with a Berkley, along with my Heddon rods, for a number of years.

$35+

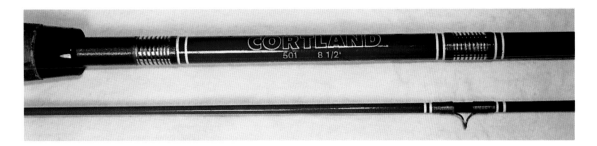

Cortland Model 501 glass fly rod

two-piece, 8 1/2', same as the handle shown in group photo earlier. It is a beautiful early glass rod.

$75+

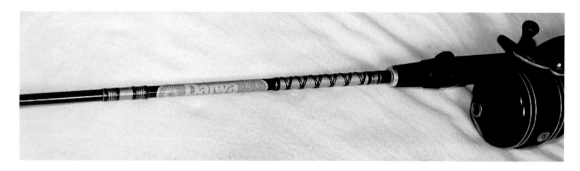

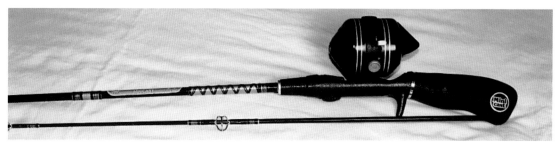

Daiwa "Mini-Cast" glass rod

with Zebco 606 Spin-cast reel (closed face spinning reel). Daiwa has been my choice for ultra light rods since the late 1960s and they perform well. This is about as modern as one would ever consider for collecting, but is a neat little rod.

$25 set

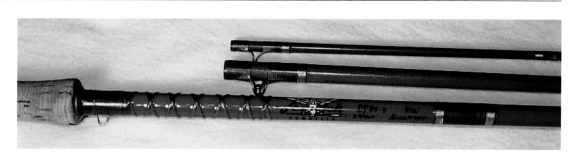

Fenwick FF85-3 glass fly rod

three-piece, 8 1/2', 3/1, 3 3/4 ounce, line #7DT in excellent condition. Note the ferrule construction.

$150+

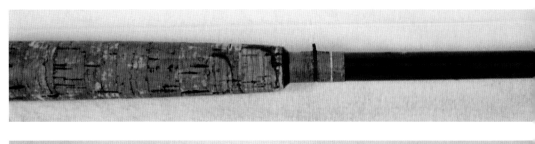

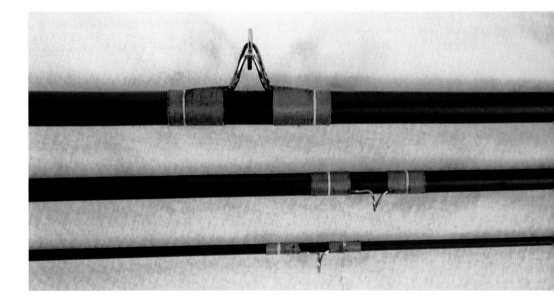

Unmarked Fenwick blanks

three-piece spinning rod. Fenwick made rods for a number of companies, including Herter's, and also sold blanks for rod kits and rod makers. These are Fenwick blanks with metal ferrules on an unmarked spinning rod. Fenwick blanks alone are valuable.

$75+

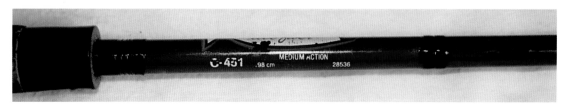

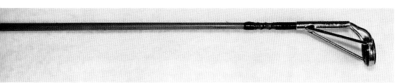

Garcia C-451 spinning rod

two-piece, serial #28536.

$75+

Garcia FC ultra light rod

two-piece Four Star.

$50+

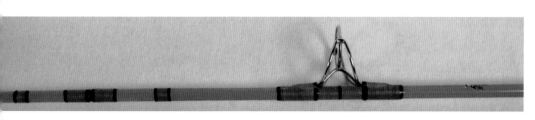

Model 50 Great Lakes "Whirlaway" rod/reel combination

This is a current "hot collectible" selling rapidly and well, online and at shows. These unique rod/reel combinations are from the early 1950s. They combined the new technologies of fiberglass rods and spinning reels into a single outfit.

$75-$125

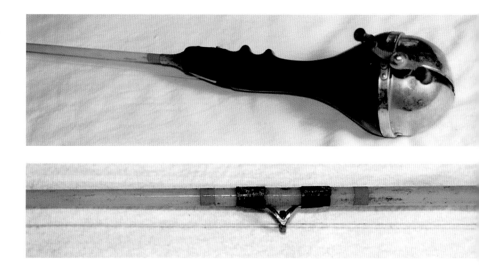

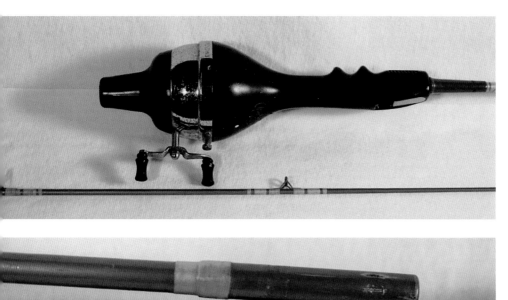

Model 75 Whirlaway

showing some of the details. This is a more difficult model to find than the Model 50 and is in excellent condition.

$125+

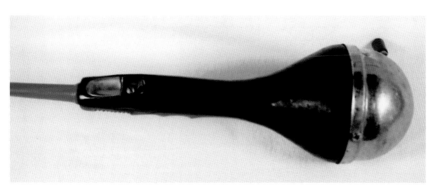

Model 50 Whirlaway combos

one open, showing part of the reel mechanism. They are in rougher condition.

$50-$75

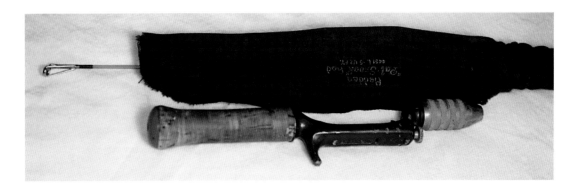

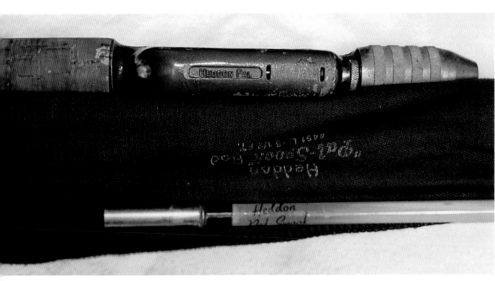

Heddon Pal Spook

#4451, 5 1/2' glass casting rod in original case, all matching to serial number (a metal Pal is shown later).

$175+

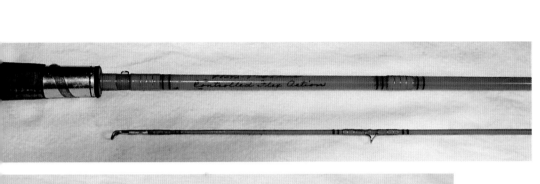

Heddon Golden "Mark 50" Pro Weight glass fly rod

two piece, 7', with the Heddon "controlled flex" action and a tube from the same era. See my Golden Mark pack rod later in this chapter, purchased in 1968. I personally think that these are the finest rods ever made by Heddon. I still fish with my fly rod and my casting rod.

$200+

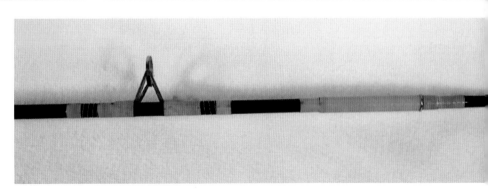

Johnson Uni-Spin

earliest model, after getting the rights from Tru-Temper. It is nearly identical to the Tru-Temper version with metal ferrules. This rod is a lot of fun to use and I still cast for pike with my Tru-Temper version.

$50-$75

Johnson Uni-Spin

second model with fiberglass ferrules, likely after acquiring the Philipson line of rods. Any of the Philipson/Johnson rods are very collectible and are extremely well-made glass rods. This rod is in excellent condition and works great.

$100+

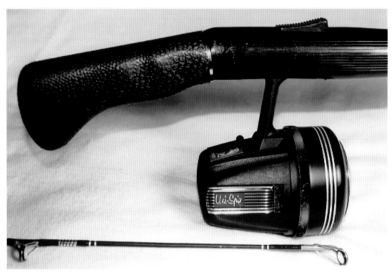

Langley Model 5485

two-piece 8 1/2' fly rod, metal ferrules, Fenwick blanks, in its original sock.

$100+

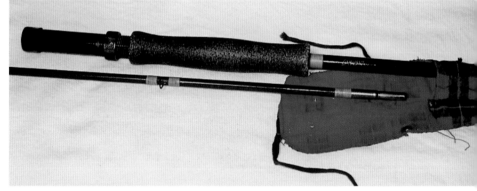

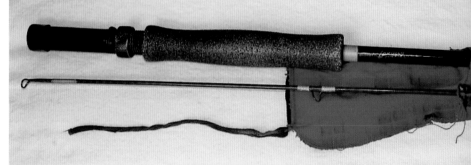

Montague Model 3753 SL casting rod

named Clear Lake. As I grew up on Clear Lake in Kent County, Mich., this rod is rather special to me. It has pretty gold line guides and wrapping trim. Montague was one of the largest producers of rods and reels in America. Dozens of reels are shown in the next chapter.

$25+

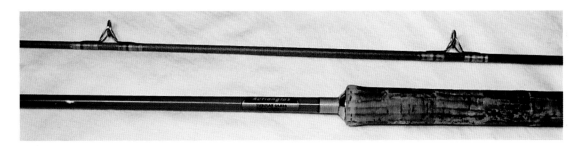

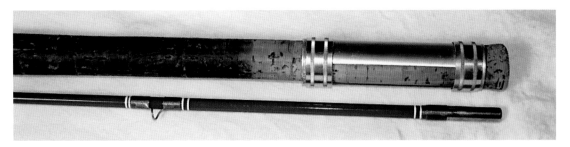

Orchard Industries Actionglas two-piece spin/fly rod

One photo shows the details of the handle designed for either spinning or fly-fishing, but the tip is actually a Cortland as shown earlier in this section. The correct tip is in the photo with the multicolor wraps.

$50+

Case for Model 1270-T fly Wonderod

by Shakespeare, 7' 9". The "Howald" process is named for the inventor of the innovative fiberglass rod-making process that changed the rod-making industry forever. The spiral glass design is obvious when one examines a Shakespeare rod closely, as shown later.

$20+

Shakespeare Model 1577-L Wonderod

casting rod, 6', and correct sock. The Model FCJ is actually a dating code used by Shakespeare on its glass rods (similar code used on reels). On the rods, the first two letters indicate the year from a code chart, with A being 0 and M being 12 and the third letter is the month using the same code. This rod was made in February 1958.

$20+

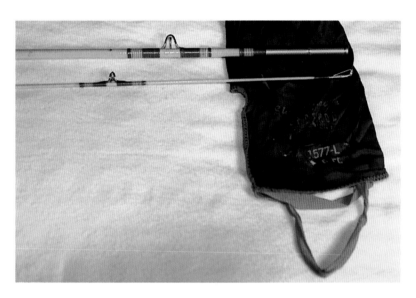

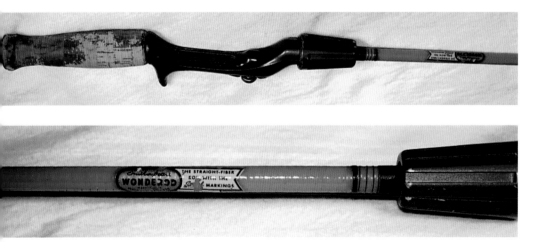

Wonderod by Shakespeare

less expensive model. This green glass version does not have the coding on it.

$10+

Shakespeare Model 1587-M

Wonderod casting rod, 6', with date code of FBM, meaning December 1959. The L in the one earlier stands for light and the M in this one stands for medium action.

$75-$125

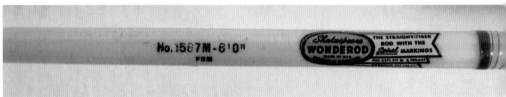

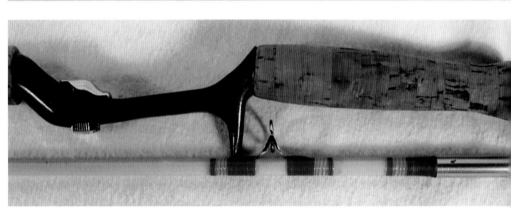

Shakespeare Professional spinning Wonderod

Model 940XX, 6' with date code of EDF, meaning May 1967.

$50+ as it is rougher

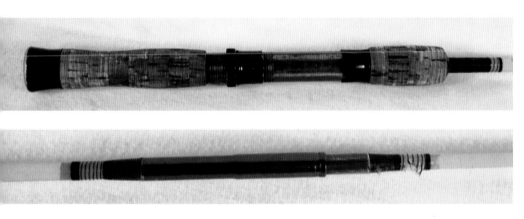

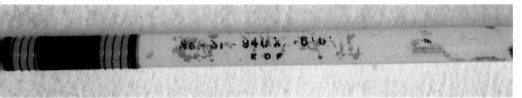

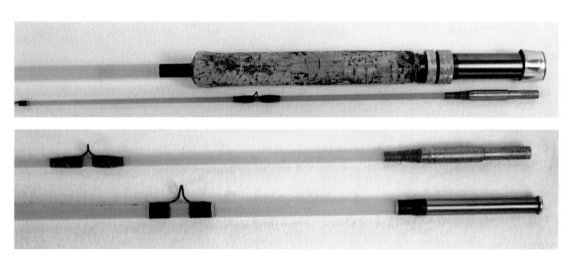

Shakespeare Wonderod fly rod

two-piece, line guide and male ferrule rewrapped as tip was apparently broken. Rod is about 7', likely a 7 1/2' originally.

$25+ due to condition

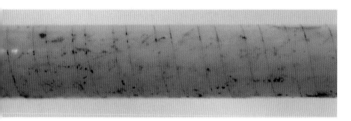

Shakespeare Wonderod casting rod

Model No. B-412M, 5' 2" long, found in an estate sale with nice Shakespeare President Model 1970 casting reel dated 1947 (reel code GD). Close-ups show the wrapping and the "spiral glass design" of the Howald Process.

Rod, $75-$125
Reel, $150-$200

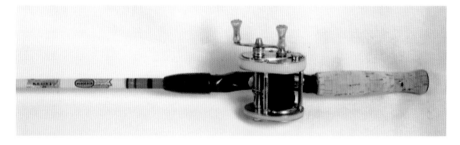

South Bend Outdoorsman Model spinning rod

from the South Bend/Gladding era, toward the end of South Bend as a manufacturer (the company currently only imports rods/reels and terminal tackle; the Oreno line is owned by Luhr Jensen).

$25+

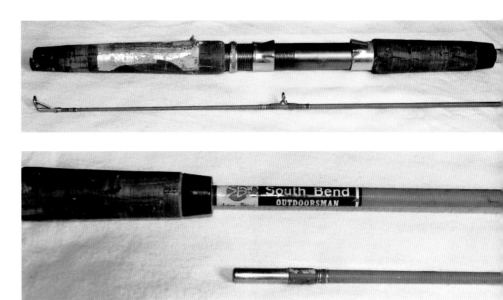

South Bend glass fly rod

Model 3123, 9', 3/1, complete handle is shown in the group shot at the beginning of this section. This is from the 1950s when South Bend still used the "A Name Famous in Fishing" logo, as seen on the rod under the company name and above the model number.

$50+

South Bend imported spinning rod

Model 2345 Graphite Composite, medium action with ceramic line guides. A beautiful little imported rod for 1/4- to 1/2-ounce lures.

$30+

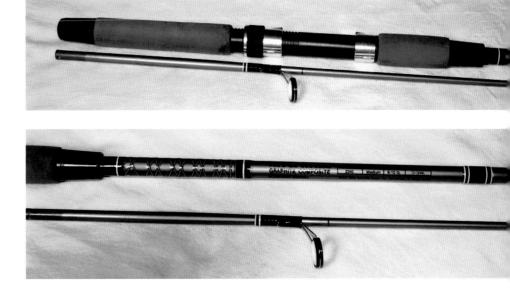

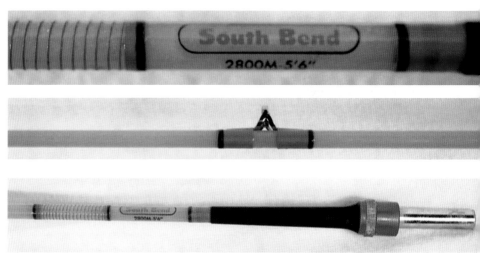

South Bend casting rod

Model 2800M, 5' 6", and correct sock. This gorgeous glass rod from the early 1950s was a top of the line model. One could use one of the universal South Bend handles and exchange rod blanks, depending on the action desired.

$150+

South Bend Surf/ Ocean rod

Model Deluxe 50660 in glass, showing details of wrapping and tip. A sticker saying solid brass marks the reel seat and it is also stamped South Bend. There is little collector interest at this time for these rods, especially away from the coasts, so they may be a good thing to start saving.

$20+

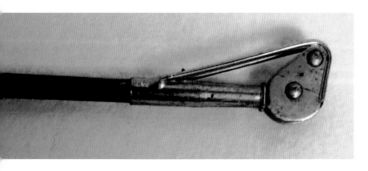

True Temper Dynamic metal casting rod

with an early Super Zebco and an unmarked glass rod likely made for Ward's using the Sport King logo (made by Richardson?). True Temper by American Fork & Hoe was one of the most successful of metal rods jobbed to wholesalers all over America and the ones with the SpeedLock Grip, as shown, are very collectible, and usable. These two rods/reels have a little story behind them. I was asked to advise the prop manager for the new Fox movie called I Walk the Line, the story of Johnny Cash, regarding typical tackle from 1955 for a scene when Johnny met June Carter in a hardware store. These two rods/reels were to be used in the movie, as they are typical from the 1955 era, but a number of factors created complications. The prop manager was lucky enough to find what he needed, based upon my advice and photos of these, in an old sporting goods store in Nashville. They are valued at $75+ each with the reels; each rod alone is worth $35-50+ depending on age and condition. A mint example of the Dynamic sold online for $112 a couple of years ago.

Rods, $35-$50+; with reels, $75+ each

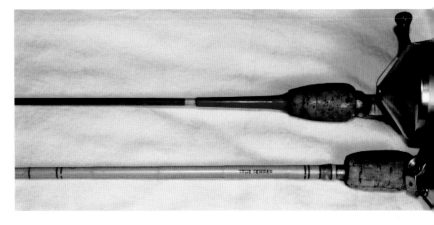

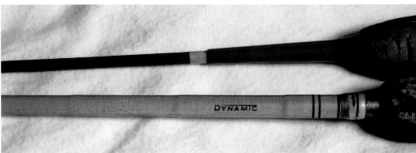

True Temper heavy glass trolling rod

for the Great Lakes or oceans. This one hangs over one of my photo studio areas. There is not a lot of collector demand for these right now, but this pristine rod is worth $25-$50 at least.

$25-$50

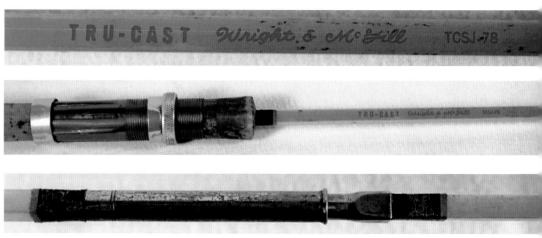

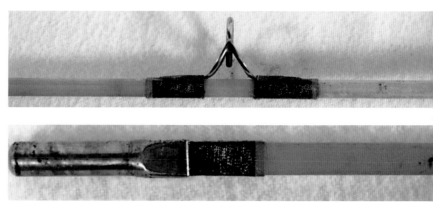

Wright & McGill Tru-Cast

square glass fly/spin combination, Model TCSJ-78. Photos also show close-ups of ferrules and guides for identification purposes on these unique square rods. This is a very early 1950s W & M rod.

$35+

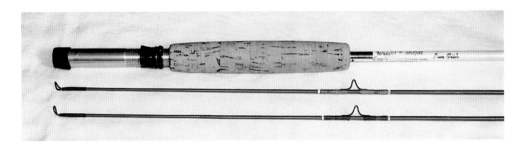

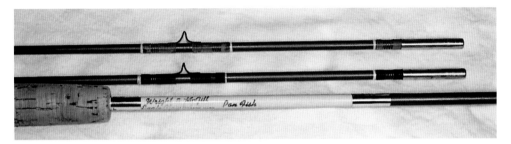

Early Wright & McGill

2/2 Pan Fish glass fly rod, Eagle Claw name brand.

$50+

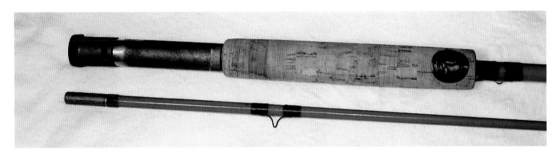

Classic Wright & McGill Eagle Claw glass fly rod

two piece. Champion model, 7 1/2', Model number 3A.

$75+

Ice Rods, Jigging Sticks and Tip-ups

Ice fishing rods have little following outside of the North. But this is a fascinating side collection to rod collecting. Ice rods were first made in bamboo and metal. Then, as with other rods, fiberglass became an important material for ice rods. One great thing about ice rods is that often one finds a small raised pillar or early multiplier reel still mounted on it as shown below. In addition to the rods, ice anglers use jigging sticks for both fishing and spearing, and tip-ups for automatic ice fishing. Collectors are just now noticing these items, but interest will continue to grow, especially for company items such as the Arnold tip-ups shown. See also the nice ice rod/reel combination in Chapter Five.

Wooden-handled metal ice fishing rod

with old Montague multiplier taped onto it.

$35 with reel

Stubby type reels

were often used for ice fishing and for lowering decoys for spearing. This one has very heavy line similar to a small rope.

$50+

St. Croix Model 40

3' 6" ice fishing rod called the Pacemaker. This beautiful little rod was made in Park Falls, Wis., by the famous glass rod maker and it is near mint. See the next entry also.

$25+

Betts Fishing Tackle Model 2205 casting rod

This is not an ice rod, but it was also made by St. Croix in Park Falls, Wis. Note the two rings around the blanks on both rods.

$25+

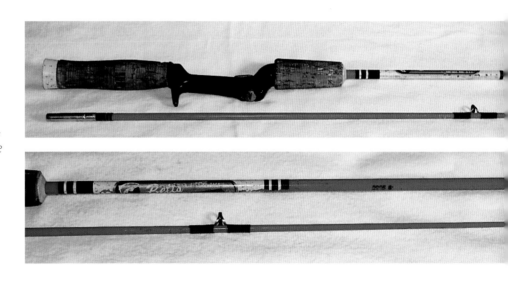

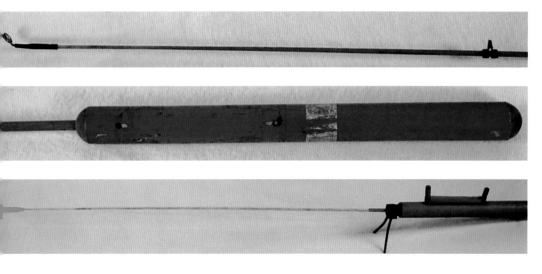

Ice rods

in 1950s style, wooden handled/glass blank.

$5-$10 each

A variety of ice rods

with a nice older wooden one in front and two walking stick/ice rod combinations next to it. The little wooden cap stays on while fishing to protect the angler from the sharp point used for walking on ice.

$5-$25 each

Target Tackle ice rod

from Bay City, Mich. Most ice rods are not marked and are very generic. The center rod in the photo at left is from Target Tackle in Bay City, which is on Saginaw Bay and has a great ice fishery.

$5-$10 each

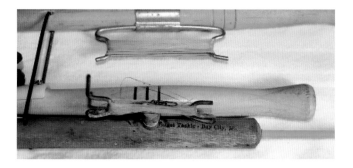

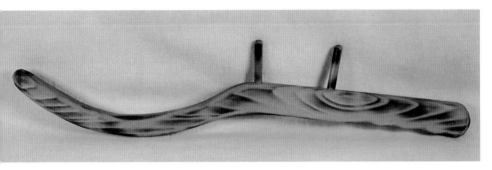

Big Bay de Noc jigging stick

Another great ice fishery is Big Bay de Noc on northwestern Lake Michigan. This is a common design used by local ice anglers and for those who spear for decoy lowering and swimming. Shown next to it is a Bear Creek sucker minnow ice decoy from Kaleva, Mich., now Ice King Decoys from Hastings, Mich. The decoy was found new in its bag from the 1950s in a tackle shop near the bay.

Stick, $10+; decoy, $30+

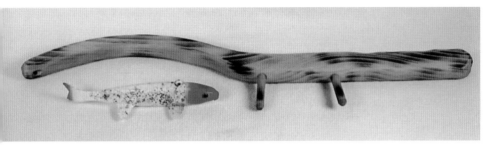

Jigging stick

nicely made, and line holder next to an unknown Upper Peninsula ice decoy.

Stick, $15-$20; decoy, $75+

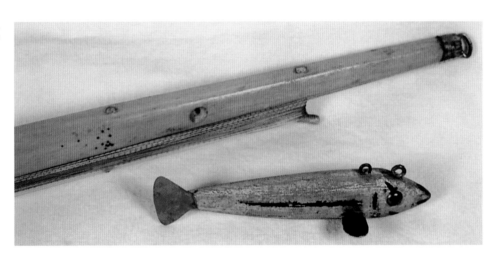

Ice rod

nicely carved, wooden handled/glass blank.

$20+

Handmade jigging device

for lake trout in Keweenaw Bay, Lake Superior, used just north of L'Anse, Mich. This was a gift from a dear friend, Ted Keranen Sr., and was made by him or his father decades ago.

$25+

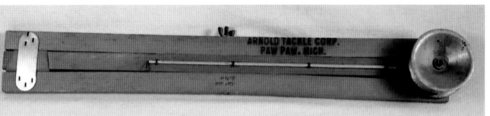

Arnold Tackle Corp. tip-up

made of wood. Arnold was purchased by Paw Paw in 1960, so these must be fairly old. The little note on it says "Butch" (the owner), 120' 12-pound line.

$50+

Slush removers

are necessities for ice fishing to keep one's hole free of ice and slush while fishing. Cast iron models are worth more.

$10+ each

Generic little ice reel

used commonly in the 1960s on ice rods.

$5+

Metal Rods

True Temper catalog

from 1941. This company was actually owned by American Fork & Hoe of Geneva, Ohio, so it should go first instead of under True Temper, as placed under glass rods. But the name True Temper is normally listed as a rod company by the glass era, so I listed it that way. The company invented the SpeedLock handle for its rods and was one of the three largest rod makers in the 1940s-50s, competing with Actionrods and Shakespeare, among others.

$75-$100 for mint 1941 catalog

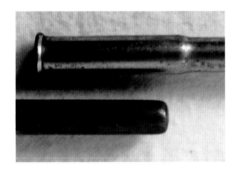

True Temper brand casting rod

showing ferrule and line guide details, SpeedLock handle. Some excellent True Temper rods have topped $100 in recent sales.

$20+ in rough shape

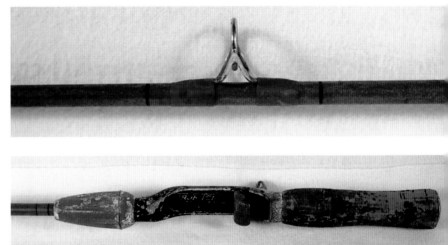

Bishoff Mfg. Co. metal rod

from Detroit, Mich. This is the only one I have ever owned. It has a great reel seat fastener that moves as it loosens the entire rod blank, e.g. the front foot holder is the rod blank itself. This is obviously a patent pending model. It was found with the Pflueger Summit mounted. Summits are common, but this one should clean up fine and is mechanically sound.

Rod, $75+; reel, $45+

Bristol extending rods

Bristol Rod from Bristol, Conn., was one of the oldest and largest of metal rod makers in America. Various examples of Bristol rods found by the author are shown. Note that one handle is rubber, some reel seats are painted and some are not. Most rods are marked on both reel seat and the lower rod blank. Rods could be used for fly reel or casting/spinning reel mounts. A simple screw reel seat fastener was used. Most of these expandable rods are not valued too highly by collectors, but if found in pristine condition are fairly valuable. The rods are plentiful, so condition is far more important.

Deluxe rubber-handled Bristol extending rod

shown mounted in casting position in excellent condition.

$50+

Two different handles

and the rod itself, one in fly-fishing position.

$25+

Nice green Bristol

in original paint in excellent condition.

$35+

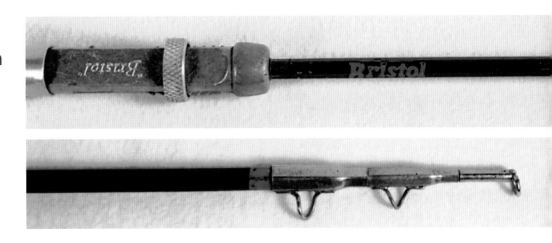

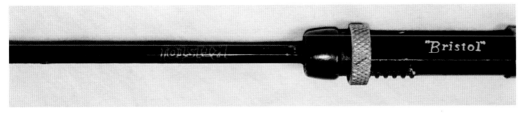

Bristol

with all original paint and painted reel seat.

$50+

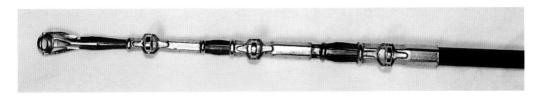

Gep metal rod

with agate guides, "Square Caster." Gephart was another large producer of metal rods in the 1930s and 1940s, but did not make the transition into glass rods as well as some other companies.

$35+

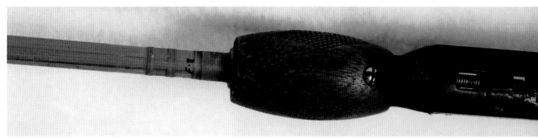

Heddon Pal baitcasting rod

#3151, F-8, in metal, 5' long. The metal is painted to look like bamboo and the line guides have agate inserts. The butt end has a rubber protector and the forehand is made of walnut with carved patterns.

$150-$200+

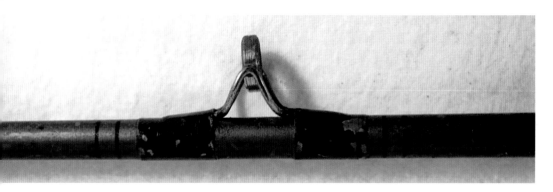

Horrocks-Ibbotson

(H-I) Super Empire alloy steel trolling rod.

$25-$40

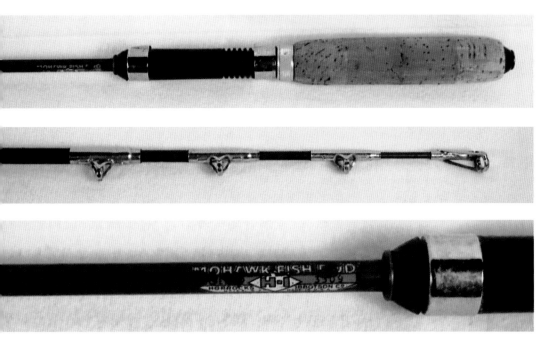

H-I Mohawk Fish Rod

extendable rod based upon a design similar to the Bristol rods shown earlier. Note the nice brass ring at the opening for the rod blank on both ends of the grip.

$50+

Hurd Super Caster

like new with hang tag. Hurd rods made in Detroit, Mich., in the late 1940s and early 1950s are very collectible and currently sell for $150-$225. They originally came in a carrying case similar to a gun case. The cow is using a cane pole and not a Hurd.

$150+

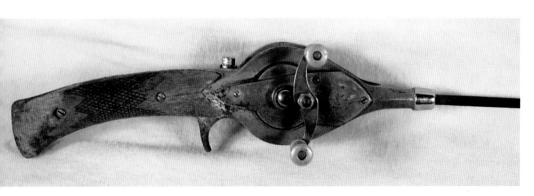

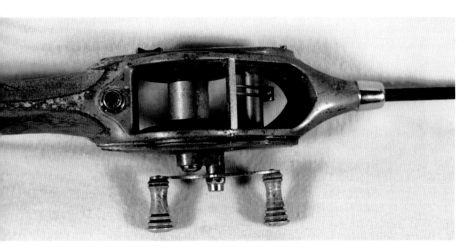

A Hurd

in rough shape shows the reel details.

$50+

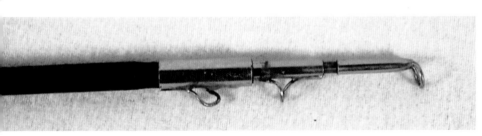

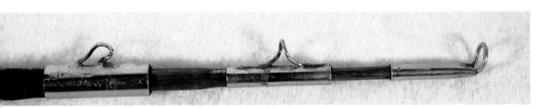

J. C. Higgins extending rod

Made for and sold only by Sears, Roebuck & Co., this is likely a Richardson rod (see page 59). See the reel chapter for many J.C. Higgins reel examples.

$25+

Orchard Industries Action Rod

made for Sears in the "Ted Williams" model, along with a Ted Williams casting reel. This rod is valuable due to the Ted Williams name and the fact that it is an Action Rod. The reel is selling for extremely high prices at this time.

Rod, $150+; reel, $250+

Premax casting rod

I had not seen this one until recently. It is a little solid steel rod made in Niagara Falls, N.Y., by Premax Products. It has some wear to the metal reel seat, but the decal is sound and the cork is in excellent shape.

$10-$20

Richardson Rods

of Chicago was another one of the largest metal rod makers competing strongly with Bristol and Gep. Shown are some very old and newer Richardson rods, showing the details. The company made both solid and tubular metal rods, and also made extending rods similar to the Bristol type.

Richardson square solid steel rod

with cork handle and agate guides. This is an older model and the handle is in rough shape, but it is a nice rod.

$10+ (more if excellent)

Champion Model extending rod

by Richardson with agate guides. It is a Patent Applied For model, an early one.

$40+

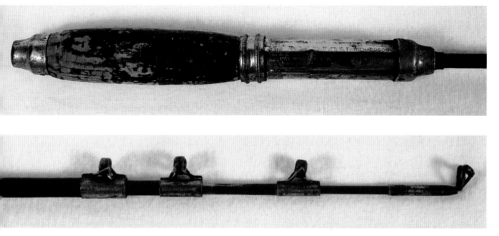

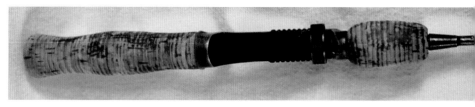

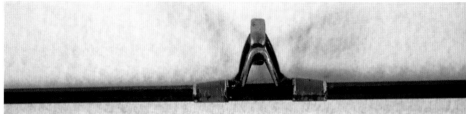

Solid steel Richardson

with agate guides and nice cork. The reel seat shows the common trademark.

$40+

Older trademark

saying Richardson Rod & Reel Company, with the triangle only over the R. Extension rod with reversible cork handle. The cork is nearly ruined.

**$10+ like this,
$40+ if excellent.**

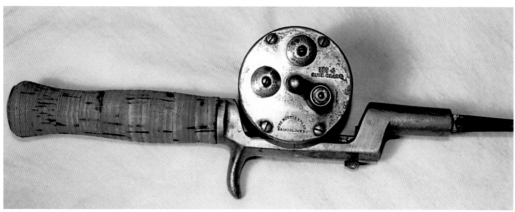

Older square Richardson rod

with perfect cork and agate guides with a Meek No. 4 Blue Grass mounted on it. This is a Horton Meek from Bristol, Conn., and the handle is missing. However, it is not a bad garage sale find. The reel works perfectly and has not been cleaned.

Rod, $50+; reel, $400+

Newer Richardson trademark

once they used plastic reel seats, but still a solid steel rod. Based on the reel seat fastener mechanism, the Sport King shown with the Dynamic True Temper glass rod earlier may have been made by Richardson.

$10

Union Hardware extending rod

with agate guides, from Torrington, Conn.

$25+

Sunnybrook casting rod

by Union Hardware. Sunnybrook was also a name for a popular Union Hardware reel that we shall see in the next chapter. The finger grip is broken and kept on by silk line.

$35+

A Union Hardware handle

from a metal rod with fiberglass blank inserted by the angler.

$5-$10

Union Hardware

second type of extending rod.

$25+

Unknown but unique metal rod

This rod screws together and the reel seat is carved from the wooden stock of the handle as one integral unit. The reel seat fastener is a simple slide ring. The rod is less than 5' overall.

$50+

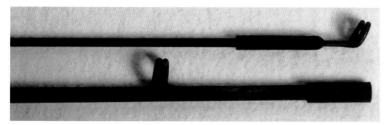

Pack and Compact Rods

Some of the extendable rods shown earlier could have been put in this category, but I am only showing a few examples of nicer glass rods, one bamboo rod, a gentleman's rod in metal and an interesting rod in Beryllium that stores in its own handle. This is a fascinating sideline to a "regular" rod collection.

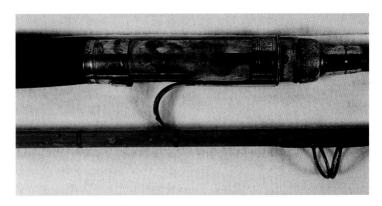

Antique bamboo pack rod

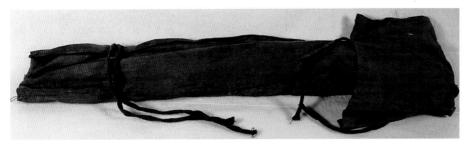

usually referred to as Gentleman's Rods. These rods were designed for the traveler, so angling was always an option. Some of the late 1800s and early 1900s advertisements show a man slipping this rod into the inside of his topcoat to be at the ready. This rod shows some of the typical problems of old bamboo rods: rewrapped in places, broken and shortened blank and others. Still, it is a nice rod for any collection.

$25+ in this shape, $100+ if intact

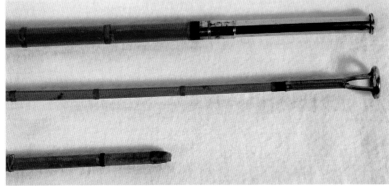

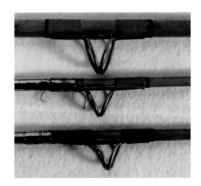

Antique metal takedown rod

not a true Gentleman's Rod, as they were usually four-piece rods. But this one is as nice as they come and I took lots of photos to show its beauty and details. It is unmarked by the maker.

$100+

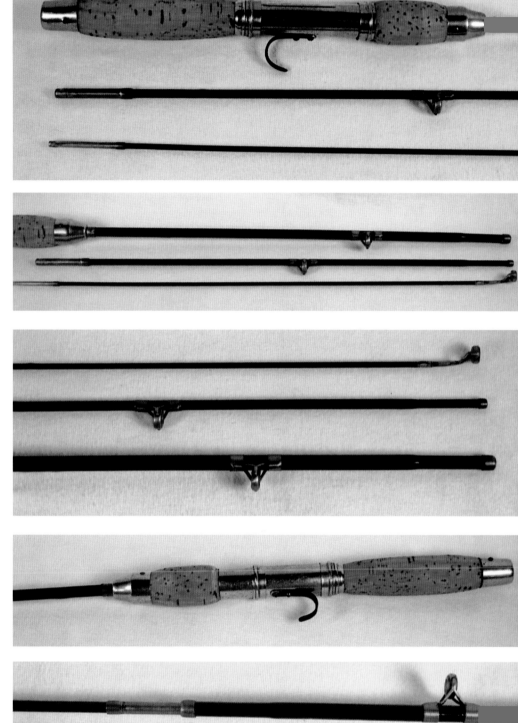

Champion Products Co.

of Muskegon, Mich., "Handle Rod" made of beryllium. This is a Patent Applied For model in mint condition with the original shipping plastic still over the cork handle.

$75+

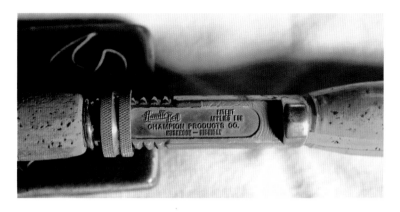

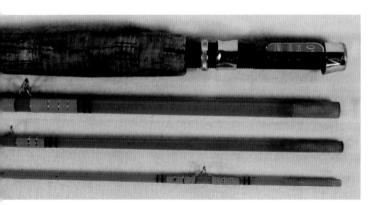

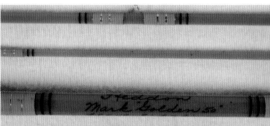

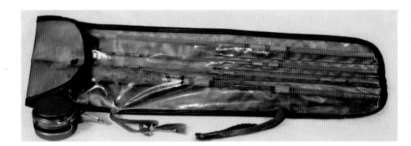

Heddon Mark "Golden 50"

3/2 pack rod #8548, 8' rod, #7 line. This is my personal rod, purchased new in 1968 and fished with ever since. The ferrules are excellent and the rod action is superb. It is a great rod for panfish and whitefish, as well as trout species of all types. I think this rod has fished in as many states as most and it shows virtually no wear on the rod itself. The reel is a Heddon Automatic fly reel also shown in the next chapter.

$200+

St. Croix fiberglass extendable cane-type rod

Not really a pack rod, but too cool to leave out of the book. This is a fiberglass replacement for the "old cane pole" of our childhood days.

$25+

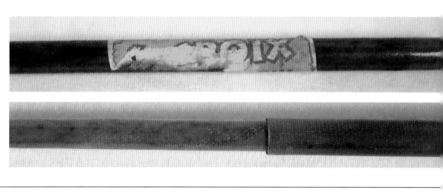

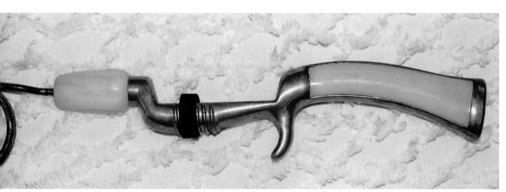

Waltco Products Stubcaster coil blank rod

designed to come apart and fit in tackle box, advertised as ideal for trolling or pier fishing by Waltco Products, Chicago. This was new in 1949.

$50+

Wright & McGill "Trailmaster"

Model No. TRP 600, 7 1/2' spin/fly combination pack rod in hard metal tube for protection.

$200+

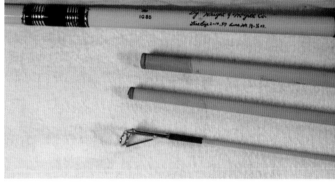

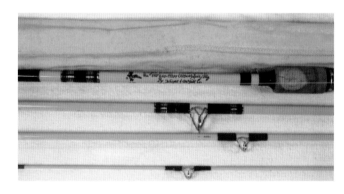

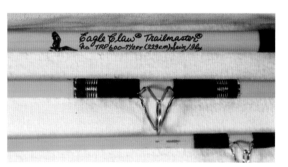

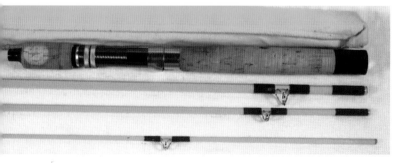

Chapter Two:
COLLECTIBLE REELS

Reels have been collected nearly as long, or maybe even longer, than lures by many individuals. During the fall of 2003, a major reel collection was dispersed in Kalamazoo, Mich., with many reels bringing hundreds of dollars each and some topping the four-figure mark. The collection also contained some lures, but they were only lures "picked up while buying reels." Not all collectors focus on lures, and many would rather collect the more substantial and mechanically operating reels.

It is no surprise to anyone who has ever held a Vom Hofe, Meek, Milam or early New York-type reel in his hands. These are truly works of the jeweler's art. To operate a

A few reels

which are seen in detail later in the book (Bronson, Meisselbach, Pflueger, Ocean City, Union Hardware).

$25-$200 each

reel more than 100 years old that is still smooth as silk is a real joy. Other reasons collectors are now turning toward reels in greater numbers are due to their availability and oftentimes lower cost than comparable lures. When I first really started to expand my collection about a decade ago, most collectors ignored any reel unless it was at least 75 years old. One could easily buy 1940s-60s reels for $5 each or less. This is no longer true, as collectors have learned the true value of reels. They often sell now for four to six times that price for even the common Shakespeare, Pflueger or similar models. Another new area of interest is in spinning reels. As with lures, the spinning era of reels has only been discovered by most collectors in recent years.

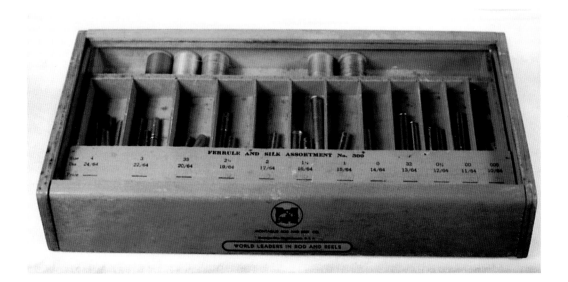

The value of a reel is determined by its appearance and its working condition. This is up to each collector to judge. However, I certainly think that reels in great working order should be valued higher than those that are perfect in appearance, but do not work. Missing parts, replaced cranks and screws, damaged screws and soldered foots lower the value of a reel. Of course, how a reel has been cared for will determine its value as well. Collectors are far more interested in an old Meek with original patina than one cleaned inappropriately. The addition of boxes, wrenches, papers, parts lists and oilers will also increase the value of a reel. Most collectors prefer that one not clean a reel, if it is going to be offered for sale, as the patina is often harmed by harsh chemicals or polishing. Of course, one should clean reels for one's own collection in any fashion desired. However, if you find a Meek with beautiful patina, it would be my personal recommendation to leave it alone. So what are the areas to watch for in a reel?

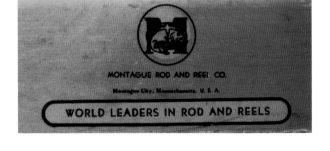

Montague Rod & Reel Co. dealer display

of ferrules and rod repair lines. Rare.

$400+

1. **Mechanical condition.** Reel collectors usually use a 1-10 scale on working condition. If rated a 10, the reel should work perfectly.

2. **Appearance.** Reel collectors also use a separate 1-10 scale to grade a reel on its appearance. A rating of 10 indicates the reel is in mint/new condition.

3. **Parts.** All reels are devalued if any of the parts are missing or have been replaced. This includes screws, the reel foot, line guides, jewels, end caps and level wind mechanisms.

4. **Wear.** Many reels have "boat rash" on the rims caused by bumping and rubbing in the boat or while in storage. This is part of the grading on appearance, but should always be noted when selling or buying a reel.

5. **Marring.** Collectors greatly downgrade the condition of a reel if any of the screws have been bent, scratched or marred by attempts to remove them or during repairs. This is also true if other items on the reel are marred.

6. End caps. End caps, including any jewels, need to be present and original. This would include original star washers on Vom Hofe reels and similar drag accessories.

7. Reel foot. All reels have a "foot" that fits into the "seat" of a rod. Many very old reels have had the foot soldered and/or altered in some way. Many times the foot has been shortened to fit a particular reel seat and this would harm the value. Also, many old small Hendryx-type reels have had two small holes drilled into the reel foot to allow them to be screwed onto ice fishing rods in the north. As a collector of early Hendryx, Vom Hofe and Montague reels, I have often been disappointed when finding a premier reel with two holes in the seat. Any soldering or alteration greatly depreciates the value of the reel.

Bronson Mercury

No. 2550 with great fishing scenes stamped into end plates. These were not expensive reels, but sure were pretty. A similar J. C. Higgins that is shown later in this chapter has even more detailed engraving, simply beautiful.

$20-$25

8. Patina. This is, of course, not an original element of the reel. It is a natural aging function of the reel interacting with the air. Original glowing patina on a 100-plus year old reel is beautiful and should be left alone. A nice patina will only add value to the reel. Buffed, polished and scratched reels will lose value in the eyes of most collectors.

9. Click. Most reels have a "click" mechanism that functions to slow the reel down and is a replacement for a drag on some reels. Collectors normally grade a reel's click mechanism in two ways: strength of click mechanism internally while the reel is being used and ease of how the clicker itself works.

10. Rarity. Of course, the greatest value condition is the rarity of the reel itself. An early Vom Hofe, Meek, Milam, Conroy and others has no comparison in value to most reels by the major lure companies of the 1900s. However, some early Shakespeare reels are worth thousands of dollars. The top sale in the 2003 Kalamazoo reel auction was a rare and early Shakespeare.

Reels are also usually sorted by type. Many of the early reels were little more than line retrievers that would later be emptied onto a line dryer (see examples of line dryers later in the book) to keep the silk line from rotting. However, eventually reels were manufactured for a specific type of fishing: trolling, casting, fly-fishing, spinning, larger saltwater versions and some interesting combination reels. Many collectors concentrate on only one type while others will collect any reel of interest. Most collectors ignored spinning reels until the past few years, but the interest in them is now keen. There are also rod/reel combinations that are very collectible, such as the Chicago and Hurd rods.

Reels in this book are shown in great detail to assist the collector in identification of unknown reels and to show the importance of small differences in even the more common company reels. Identification of reels is one of the greatest challenges to the collector. There has been little reliable data generally available until the recent advent of a few Internet sites that truly are invaluable to the collector. Many of the early collector books had major errors about company information. It becomes further confusing because many companies were bought and sold a number of times, often with only minor changes in the reels being made and distributed. Hendryx was sold to Winchester, Meek to Horton, Meisselbach to Bristol. One of the most common errors regarding the name "Pennell" is thinking it was a company. It was merely a trademark of the Edw. K. Tryon Company of Philadelphia, Pa., an early and major distributor of rods, reels, tackle and lures. The Tryon Company had many trademarks for its lures, lines and other items that were made for it by major companies. Pennell is found on reels made by many companies, including Montague and Vom Hofe.

In addition, many of the major manufacturers of early reels, such as Edward Vom Hofe, would also sell reels made by other companies and stamp their names on some reel part, such as the crank. A reel is shown later that appears to be a Montague, but is marked Edward Vom Hofe. So, the company one would believe at "first blush," when examining a reel, is the manufacturer is not always the maker. Many unscrupulous sellers are taking advantage of this fact online by claiming reels to be something they are not, so beware. There are at least three Internet sites that are indispensable to the reel collector. The best is the one owned and maintained by author and reel collector Phil White at ***www.oldreels.com***. The details offered to collectors of reels on this site are amazing. White's sections on manufacturers, identification and common reel names are wonderful and should be examined in detail by anyone serious about fishing reel collecting. His section on identification by reel foot style is superb and will quickly help one learn a Pflueger from a Hendryx, for example. White also owns and maintains

www.oldfishingstuff.com. This site has collectible tackle of all types, giving reel history, company identification and most importantly links to other sites with reel sales data. Finally, the growth in interest in spinning reels will only increase partly due to the wonderful site now available to all at **http://www.oldfishingstuff.com/ spinreel_report.htm**. This is part of White's site, but is furnished generously by collector Ben Wright, an early and major collector of spinning reels. He has compiled sales data from online sales that is very detailed and complete for spinning reels, and some other reels as well. Finally, White has included major links to other sites of interest, including the club known as Old Reel Collectors Association (ORCA). ORCA is a club dedicated to the furtherance of knowledge and collecting of reels. A collector should join if interested in maintaining current information about reel collecting. Of course, the National Fishing Lure Collectors Club (NFLCC) also has a site. It is dedicated to reel collecting as a part of its interest in lure collecting and history. There are also sites dedicated to European reels and collectors, early spinning reels, particular brand names and more. A "virtual trip" to **www.oldreels.com** will keep one busy for days, reading and sampling reel collecting around the world.

White was one of the first serious reel collectors that I was lucky enough to meet early in my reel collecting. I cannot thank him enough for his willingness to share information at shows and online. This resource is just too good to miss. Not all reels are identifiable at this time. Many of the earliest brass reels are very similar and some may be English rather than American. Early ones with horn, bone and ivory crank knobs are beautiful and likely date from the mid-1800s. However, it is not always possible to identify them with precision. Two early types were the Terry reels and the Kopf patented foot reels. We are still learning about this period and I am sure more information will come forward to help us better identify these beautiful little reels. Not knowing the exact maker does not detract from the value of these early reels.

One of the first major reel makers in America was the Hendryx company. It also made early metal lures that make a fine addition to the reel collection. Hendryx made bird cages and other metal objects as well in the later half of the 1800s, and started producing reels after receiving an 1886 patent. An advertisement appearing in 1900 claimed that the company had already sold 2 million reels in 18 years. This would indicate that major production began in 1887 or 1888. Most of the early Hendryx reels were "line gatherers" and not reels as we would think of them today. However, it also produced early fly reels and multipliers. The stamped metal reels without a click are common, but the multipliers and any of the hard rubber reels are scarce. It is not unusual for the first raised pillar reel in any collection to be a Hendryx-made reel.

Montague is also a common reel to find. However, as with the Hendryx reels, the better Montague reels are far scarcer and have skyrocketed in value. The hard rubber/German silver fly reels, as beautiful as any, no longer sell for $30-$50 as was common five years ago. Montague also jobbed reels through many sources, and one will find many marked Pennell that were sold by Tryon. It also furnished reels to many other jobbers and wholesalers as well as some major reel makers.

Three Pflueger items

(Progress reel, box and sinker) and some Heddon dealer dozens of River Runts from 1947-48 and Deep-6 from the 1960s. Values: reel, $30-$40; box, $30-$40; sinker, $10-$20; Heddon cases $600-$1,000 each, based upon actual sales in 2004.

$10-$40 each for Pflueger items

Pflueger, the Enterprise Manufacturing Company, was the major player in reel production from the early 1900s until being merged with Shakespeare in 1960. Shakespeare was Pflueger's major competitor in the 1920s-1950s, and the merger of the two companies brought one era to an end. Many early Pflueger reels are not marked except for yardage on the foot. Pflueger also used the trade name of "Portage" on many of its early raised pillar reels. It also used the name "Four Brothers" on early reels, including the hard rubber fly reels and baitcaster shown later in this chapter. The invention of the Pflueger Supreme was a landmark in reel-making history, and the reel made the company both famous and financially sound for many years. There are many evolutionary stages to the Supreme and one will find numerous variations in the field. The early Supremes were selling for more than $25 in the 1930s, making them rather expensive then and harder to find today. Pflueger produced many, many reel types and models, with the Summit, Nobby and Akron being a few. The Summit is actually one of the prettiest of all baitcasting reels, with its decorative stamping on the plates.

Other significant contributions to reel history include the famed Kentucky Reel types made by Meek, Milam, Horton and others, and the early New York-style reels with ball handles by Conroy and others. Carlton was in business only a few years, but made beautiful reels. The Meisselbach company history has been thoroughly researched and documented by Phil White in his book on the company, and the reels are in great demand today.

Spinning reels became important beginning in the 1940s. Returning service personnel brought home early spinning reels, rods and lures from the European Campaign. Airex was our first major producer of spinning reels, with the Bache-Brown reels that were soon thereafter purchased by Lionel, the toy train giant. Garcia Mitchell reels were among the first major European invasions. They

Fishing collectibles

shown in this book. A few of the many hundreds of items include: fish basket on the top row; green book that was a gift to O. L. Weber on second shelf; Montague display case; Frost advertising plate; Falls City tackle box on the bottom shelf; Meeks, Montague Reels, Pflueger Reels, Vom Hofe Reels, Yale Reels and more.

$10-$2,000 each

Ambassadeur 5000

serial number 730802, raised metal on foot, pearl double handle, three-screw .

$200-$250

eventually won the contest with American anglers, and the Model 300 became one of the most popular reels in history. Other significant European reels included the Swiss contribution of the Record, and the Abu Cardinal of later years.

The postwar era of the 1950s saw the eventual introduction of many Japanese baitcasting, fly and spinning reels. I have shown a wide selection of these reels made for general distribution and some made specifically for Ward's or Sears. The other significant historical event of the 1950s was the popularity of the Abu Ambassadeur reels that were introduced to America.

These reels are beautiful, superbly made, easy to use and still in demand for fishing as well as collecting. The Model 5000 set the stage for many others to come. I still recall studying catalogs in the 1950s, dreaming of one day owning an Abu Ambassadeur 5000. This nostalgia contributes to all collecting interests and it, along with the quality of these reels, has driven the prices to unheard of levels in recent years. Many Ambassadeur reels command $200 plus and the presentation models in the wooden boxes sell for thousands of dollars. Hi Speed models also usually command a premium, as do models with unusual crank configurations or other special features.

The foregoing is not a history of reels as much as a highlight of a few of the big players in reel manufacturing. Bronson became the largest in the world at one time, and the J. A. Coxe and Bronson reels will not be slighted in this book, either. Martin was an early automatic fly reel maker and many examples are shown. Reels were made for Sears and Wards. Vom Hofe reels are my personal favorites and many are included. I could not include all I have to show, due to space limitations of this book. However, nowhere does one find such large exploded views of reels. This should help the collector in learning details. As to history, many sources are available, but one of the best is a simple book on antique fishing tackle advertising called *Great Tackle Advertisements: 1874-1955,* compiled by Larry M. Smith in 1990. In this one source, collectors are able to find early advertisements for Hendryx, Meisselbach, Carlton, Cozzone, Yawman & Erbe, Heddon, South Bend, Pflueger, Shakespeare, Montague and many other classic reel makers. The book ends with 1955, as it was written before many collectors were concentrating on the 1940-1985

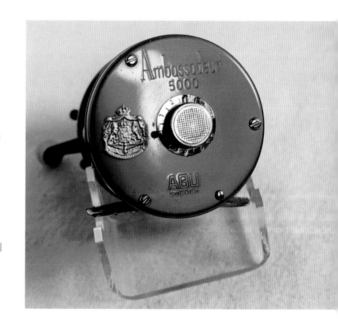

era. However, it is an excellent source of historical data, nicely compiled in one volume. With this book and the Internet sites referred to, an individual will receive a good introductory lesson in reel history.

As with lures, reels in their original boxes have increased value. Most reels were packed into a two-piece cardboard box with a cloth bag or sock, a tube of reel oil, some paperwork explaining the reel, a separate paper "parts list," sometimes a list of repair stations, maybe an extra pawl or crank or line guide, and often a screwdriver designed to repair the reel. The presence of any or all of these items increases the collectibility (and value) of the reel. The two-piece boxes became one-piece fold-over boxes in the 1960s for many reels, but the presence of the box is still important.

One nice aspect of reel collecting is the ease of displaying reels. The older boxes are often used as stands for the reels and many reels can be displayed in a small area. Also, they are ideal for shadow box displays. Regardless of one's interest in reel collecting, at least a few truly add to the beauty of a lure collection. A collection of reels can be stunning. I enjoy all of my reels. They are fun to examine periodically and I enjoy seeing them function. Also, they have a far less chance of deteriorating than a wooden lure with fragile paint from 90 years ago.

As with the rod chapter, reels are shown with a few actual recent sales followed by reels listed alphabetically by maker, when known. Unidentified or unknown reels are under a single unknown category at the end of the chapter. Some collectors may know the maker of some of these reels and, if so, I would appreciate you contacting me for future volume updates. However, I attempted to limit my identifications to reels that I was at least 95 percent certain of the maker or model. I did not separate reels as to type, e.g. baitcasting versus fly, as I wanted to list all reels by a maker together. Also, many of the early raised pillar reels were not any "type," but merely mechanisms to gather line to later be removed onto a line dryer for preservation and storage. Similarly, I have not placed reels into a set historical progression. That would be useful and interesting, but would interrupt the continuity of examining all reel types of one maker in one section. In general, the earliest reels were the solid brass reels as shown under Kopf, followed by the raised pillar style made popular by Hendryx, Pflueger and others. The hard rubber side plates are from the later 1800s and early 1900s. The Kentucky-style reels date to the mid-1800s, as do the New York-style ball handled reels. However, most of these reels are really from Horton, Montague and other companies after the 1920s. The modern level-wind was a concept dating back to the early 1900s, with the South Bend-type being one of the first and the Pflueger Supreme also being very early. Most of the reels found in collections of the more modern baitcasting type date from the 1930s-1950s. Spinning and Spin-Cast reels date from 1947 and about 1950 respectfully. Zebco was a very early manufacturer of closed face spinning reels (Spin-Cast), as was Shakespeare. The European reels such as the Mitchell and Record started showing up in large numbers in the early 1950s. The Ambassadeurs became major competitors with Pflueger and Shakespeare baitcasting reels in the mid-1950s and beyond. Japanese reels started appearing in the early 1950s in America, and became very common by the late 1950s and during the 1960s. This should give one a little sense of reel evolution.

Recent Reel Sales Data

Just a few recent sales are listed here, since most of the prices in this section are based upon actual sales. The actual sales are recorded in my own records and Lang's auction sales records.

Average baitcasting reels from the 1940s-60s will usually only bring about $20, $30-$40 if boxed. It takes a special baitcasting reel from one of the major companies to start pushing up values. It isn't always an early one, as the Bronson Invader selling for $300-$500 proves, but the early ones in general do a little better if in excellent condition. Most of the raised pillar reels start at about $20 and level off around $60 unless special. The hard rubber/German silver or hard rubber/nickled silver reels will command more than $100, and often up to $300 or more, depending on type and maker. The Meeks will easily bring from $300 to $2,000 for many models and the Vom Hofe reels sell for $100 to four-figures, depending on the reels. The Heddon German silver models do as well as comparable Meeks. Areas to watch include the increasing prices of spinning reels, as more collectors venture into this area, and some of the sleepers such as the automatic fly reels that actually date back to the 1800s. Also watch for any Bakelite reels in excellent shape, as they are generally undervalued at this time.

Lou Myer Flo-Line reel

new in the box, a very unusual reel from Wisconsin.

$75

Meisselbach Symploreel Model 972

with agate guide.

$88

Pflueger Medalist

Model 1495 fly reel.

$42

Champion Sports Equipment Co.

"Fly-Champ" fly reel with ratchet retrieve handle, built-in clicker.

$48

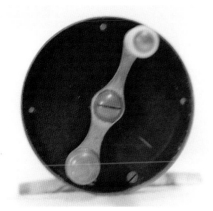

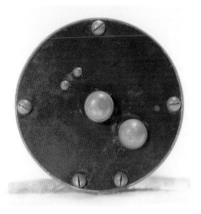

Montague fly reel

early hard rubber side plates, 40 yard. Double click mechanism, foot marked as to yards only, single counter-balanced crank, all screws perfect and no major problems with side plates.

$225+

Airex

The beginning of the American spinning reel history can be traced to Airex, and the Airex Division of Lionel, in the early 1950s. The two reel types shown were both early examples of Airex products. Note the two styles of the Bache-Brown Spinster, with the plastic added to the spool casing on the second model. Both models have the "half-bail" typical of the early spinning reels, including the earliest Mitchell reels imported from France.

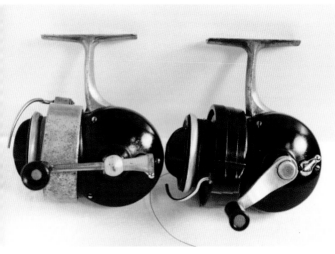

Bache-Brown Spinster reels

by Airex Division of Lionel.

$30 each

Mastereel-Spinster

Model No. 813 by Airex Division of Lionel with half-bail, drag knob removed in one photo to show company details.

$20-$25

Abu Ambassadeur of Sweden

I doubt there has been a greater recent influence on anglers or collectors regarding baitcasting reels than the beautiful and highly crafted Abu Ambassadeur reels of the 1950s-60s. These were the reels that dreams were made of for young boys in the 1950s. The reels have a high collector demand and are appreciated in Europe, Japan and America alike. I sold a red 5500 for $480+ to a Japanese collector a few years ago. There are far too many variations to show in an introductory book on reel collecting, but there are Internet sites and books available for the reels of Sweden that detail all the important minor variations. Color can be important, as can designations such as Hi Speed or number of screws holding the end plates together. The reels often came with "goodies" such as oilers and spare parts in a tube. They also are often cased in a nice leather pouch that is marked as to company. Finally, there were presentation models in wooden boxes that break the four-figure mark.

Abu also used the trade name of Garcia for its closed-face spinning reels and later acquired the Mitchell line of open-face spinning reels. In addition, beautiful glass rods were produced under the Garcia label as well as a number of lures and a large variety of other tackle. As with the Pflueger Supreme, there are many important variations in Abu reels that make them fun to collect. One could concentrate just on these fine reels for nearly a lifetime and not find them all, due to the variations.

Abu-Garcia instruction manuals

from circa 1972 showing the Ambassadeur on the left and the Cardinal on the right.

$5 each

Ambassadeur pouches

and one oiler type.

Oiler, $5; pouches $25 each in good condition

Ambassadeur 5000 and 6000 reels

Note the differences in crank configurations and the difference in the three-screw versus four-screw types on the palm side end plates. Values of $75-$200 cover most 5000-6000 reels but some of the Hi Speed models bring double that at least.

$75-$200 each

Ambassadeur 5000

serial number 730802, raised metal on foot, pearl double handle, three-screw and pouch.

$200-$250

Ambassadeur 2500C

serial number 770100, Hi Speed, raised metal on foot, single counter-balanced crank knob, pouch with slight tear and parts tube, slight rim rash, but otherwise in excellent condition.

$150-$200

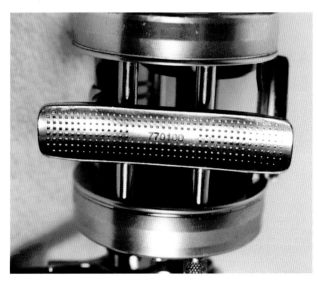

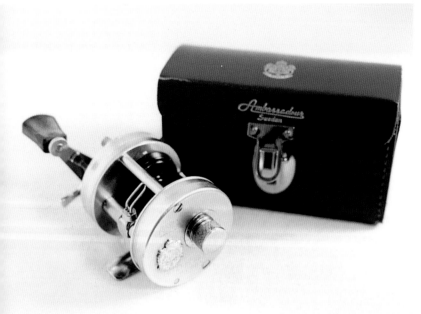

Ambassadeur 6000C

smooth foot, no serial number, three-screw, pouch and double pearl handle.

$175-$225

Ambassadeur 5600C

serial number 761100, three-screw, High Speed, double black crank knobs, raised metal on foot, thumb rest and in excellent condition without a pouch.

$125+

Details of an Ambassadeur 6000

with a smooth foot, no serial number, single counter-balanced pearl knob handle, case and reel markings on end plate. A little boat rash is on this one, but it works superbly.

$85-$125

Abu 505 spinning reel

name plate off, slight boat rash.

$100-$125

Abu-Matic 120 spin-casting reel

in beautiful gold/copper tone, about mint.

$75-$125

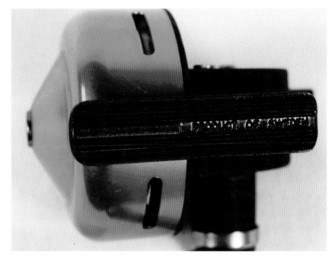

Cardinal spinning reel

later made by Zebco.

$75+

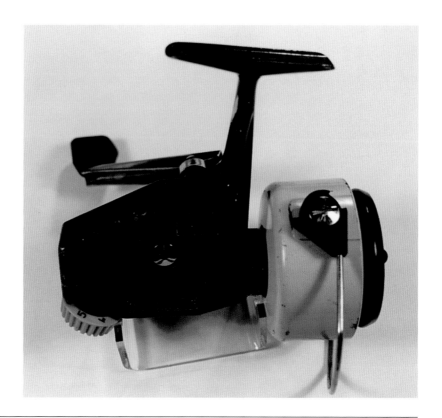

Presentation reel

given to Astronaut Frank Borman by the Garcia-Mitchell company after Apollo 8. It is a Garcia-Mitchell 408 ultra-light spinning reel. I traded his son Ed a Mason duck decoy for this new in the bag and the box reel. See more details under Mitchell. Priceless, but regular 408 models sell for $75-$150 new in the box.

No established value

Bullard & Gormley Co.

"Green Lake" baitcasting reel

with rubber end plates likely was made for this company and not by this company. It was found in an antique mall in Wisconsin in 1995. Foot marked 80 for yardage, jeweled end caps, non-level wind, counterbalanced crank, name stamped on palm side end plate.

$150+

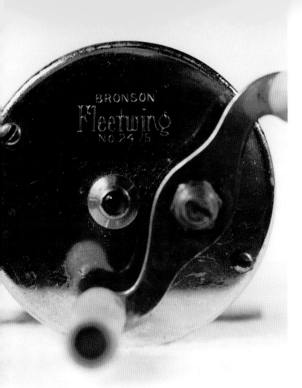

Bronson Reel Co.

Bronson Reels of Bronson, Mich., was at one time the largest producer of reels in America. In addition to its own reels, it acquired many other important producers including J. A. Coxe and Meisselbach. The company was in business from 1922 until the 1970s. It furnished everything from very inexpensive stamped metal reels to top of the line Coxe reels now selling for hundreds of dollars each. In addition, Bronson supplied many reels to Ward's, Sears, and other resale and wholesale establishments. The foot and other factors such as the oil receptacle help identify the unstamped Bronson reels made for others. However, a few Japanese reels slipped through unstamped that are Bronson copies and some of the later Ocean City reels are very similar. But, as to collector interest, it is strongest for the beautiful Coxe reels and those are easy for anyone to identify.

Bronson Fleetwing

No. 2475 showing details of the simple stamped foot found on many Bronson reels, often unmarked. This reel is a level wind with jeweled end caps, double knob crank and a single click mechanism seen on the palm end plate. This reel is well used and would not command much in the collector market, due to condition. It is a fairly common reel.

$20

Bronson Fleetwing

No. 2475 showing addition of a drag adjustment as well as the click. This one is about mint and also shows the standard foot of the later Bronson reels. This drag control and foot combination often identifies an unmarked Bronson of the 1960s era.

$20

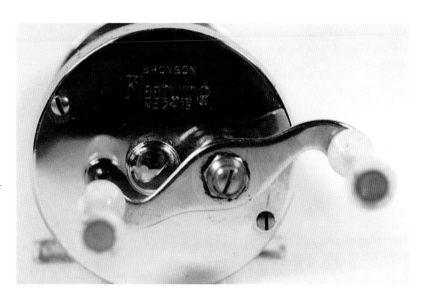

Older Bronson Biltwell

No. 2800 showing details of an early foot design and simple riveted tail plate with single click, double handle with wood knobs. Note the foot design carefully. It is similar to an early Pflueger foot, but does not have the raised center for yardage marking as on Pflueger reels. Also, the markings are: Bronson Reel Co., Bronson, Mich, Made in U.S.A. Most of the Bronson reels are marked Made in the U.S.A. if not marked otherwise. This reel is likely from the 1920s.

$20

Bronson Lashless

No. 1700, excellent in box with all papers, including hang tag. This is from late 1950s or early 1960s. Note the slight change in adjustable drag control design and the increased clicker size.

$20-$25

Bakelite Bronson level wind

unmarked, inexpensive, similar to models made by Meisselbach and others.

$5-$15

Earlier Bronson Silver Princess

No. 3700 level wind showing jeweled end caps, "s" shaped double crank with nice knobs, simple single click control, hard rubber spacer and a typical Bronson "Pat. App. For Made in U.S.A." foot marking.

$35+

Bronson Mercury

No. 2550 with great fishing scenes stamped into end plates. These were not expensive reels, but sure were pretty. A similar J. C. Higgins that is shown later in this chapter has even more detailed engraving, simply beautiful.

$20-$25

Belmont level wind

No. 3123500 with jeweled end caps and great fishing scenes likely made by Bronson for Sears, as Sears usually used a seven-digit serial number on its reels. There are no maker markings on this reel. It is missing its crank, but otherwise is in nice shape.

$20-$25

Bronson Royal Matic

390 automatic fly reel. This gorgeous fly reel was Bronson's answer to the Shakespeare OK and other types of automatic fly reels.

$30+

Bronson Dart

two versions, Model No. 95 spincast reel, two colors, otherwise identical.

$10-$12 each

Bronson Scout

No. 902 made after selling to True Temper, TT in box on foot is a trademark. Also, note the cool stylized "modernistic" foot design.

$10-$12

Bronson-made Pikie

No. 2525 level wind, made for The W. Bingham Co., Cleveland, and so stamped on head plate. This is in rough shape with screw missing and bent level wind guide, but a unique find from a particular store.

$20-$30 if in good shape

Bronson Fleetwing

No. 2475 showing a different foot style with two holes and the newer drag control. This must be the final type of the No. 2475.

$20

Bronson Lashless box

J. A. Coxe leather case and J. A. Coxe 60 C box. See reels prior and after.

Bronson/Coxe Model No. 60 C

in box with papers. This is a very nice level wind and shows the quality of some of this company's reels. Foot is stamped with Model No. 60 and it has the typical Coxe crank handle and knobs.

$60-$75

Bronson/Coxe Coronet 25

in leather pouch.

$100-$125

Bronson/Coxe Coronet N

(narrow spool).

$125+

Bronson/Coxe
Model 25-3

with wooden arbor.

$75-$125

Bronson/Coxe Model 25-2

with pouch.

$125-$150

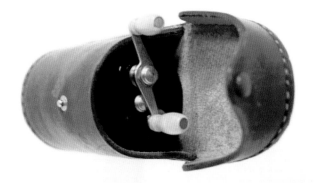

Century white Bakelite-type level wind

possible Bronson.

$5

Carleton Reels

This company had a brief history from 1903 to 1908, and then evolved into the Rochester Reel Company from 1908 until the 1920s. Any of the Carleton reels are highly desired by collectors.

Carleton Ideal fly reel

wooden knob, counter balance weight on reel spool, name stamp only on palm side. Note the foot design and click style.

$75+

Carleton Gem fly reel

name of reel and company stamped on the bottom of the horizontal reel seat. Note the clicker design. This is simply a gorgeous little reel.

$75+

English Reels

American collectors often find English reels that have migrated to America with their owners or were purchased abroad by American anglers. Many of the early antique brass reels found are actually generic English reels that simply have not been identified. The House of Hardy is one of the most desired of all reel manufacturers, but many other antique and collectible English reels exist, far too many to cover in great detail. Shown are a few fine examples of what one might find and their values.

C. Farlow & Co. Ltd.

antique 4 1/2" alloy salmon fly reel and leather case, circa 1910. This London-made fishing reel has the earlier "Holdfast" trademark with a hand carrying a large pike type fish, with the word Holdfast in the center.

$320-$400

House of Hardy Marquis

8/9 fly reel in original pouch.

$175+

Hardy Viscount

140 fly reel in box.

$125+

Edgar Sealey Flyman Model fly reel

in box, made in Redditch, also home to historic Allcock.

$50-$75

Ogden Smith antique fly reel

circa 1910, London made.

$175

Gayle Reels

This Frankfort, Ky., reel maker made some gorgeous (and valuable) Kentucky-style bait reels and this simple fly reel.

Gayle Simplicity

No. 2 fly reels.

$20-$25 each

Great Lakes Reels

This is a troublesome name, as there was a Great Lakes company that made the great rod/reel combination shown in Chapter One called the Whirlaway. It may have also made a simple level wind baitcaster. Or, the baitcaster may have been made for it by Bronson and/or Ocean City and also imported from Japan. The problem is that Great Lakes is a generic term and it may have been used by more than one company. Trademark status would be tough for this term. I show a few examples of reels that show up with the name Great Lakes.

Great Lakes Model C-60

also marked Lexington, Mich. U.S.A. on head plate, double crank knobs, foot similar to later Bronson or Ocean City, adjustable drag is similar to that of an Ocean City level wind reel. Engraved with fishing scenes, as are all of these reel types. Spacer is similar to that used on Bronson reels.

$10-$15

Nearly identical

to above but made in Japan.

$10-$15

An older Great Lakes

that I am sure is a Bronson, based upon how it is marked on the inside of the head plate the same as the Mercury and others.

$15-$20

Great Lakes Products Co. Whirlaway

Model 75 with two-piece fiberglass rod. Shown also in Chapter One.

$125+

Hawthorne (Ward's)

As with Sears, Ward's had its own brand names for lures, rods, reels and other tackle. Hawthorne and Sport King are two examples. The Sport King rod shown earlier was likely an early Ward's product. There are a number of collectors now concentrating on Ward's and Sears items. This can sometimes drive up the prices a bit. Another company made all the products, but some items were designed specifically for the big merchandisers. South Bend and Shakespeare made many of the products.

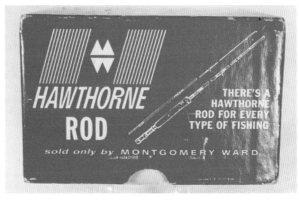

Hawthorne

Model No. 360-60-6423 vertical automatic fly reel, new in box. The box also advertises that Hawthorne rods and lines were available from Ward's.

$50

Ward's Sport King

level wind baitcaster, No. 60-6326, Model 60.

$25

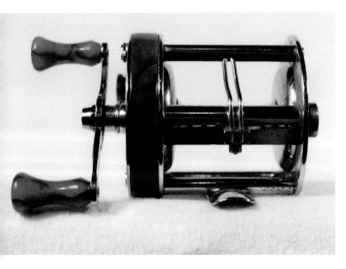

Ward's Sport King

Model 63 automatic fly reel.

$15-$20

Ward's Sport King

surf caster/ocean reel. It looks like Penn made it.

$20-$30

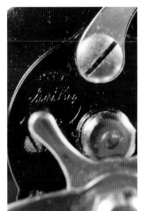

Heddon

Heddon is, of course, the number one name in fishing collectibles for most people and rightfully so, given its wonderful products and history, as well as quality of lures. Heddon also made reels and contracted for a number of reels. Although the reels were not as prolific as the lures, early Heddon Meek-style reels are superb and very valuable. The one sleeper area in Heddon collecting is likely the area of spinning and spincasting reels. These are still grossly undervalued and can often be acquired reasonably by the beginning collector. Any of the early to middle 1900s reels are very expensive and a lucky find if made in the field. Some of the better and a couple of the more common Heddon reels are shown here. A complete history of the Heddon reels and rods may be found in

Heddon Catalogs: 1902-1953, published in 2004 by Krause Publications and authored by Clyde A. Harbin Sr. and me. In this book, the entire history of Heddon is documented by actual catalog listings. The introductory years for items is given in a chart at the book's end. For instance, the 1920 catalog featured the Model 3-15, 3-24 and 3-30 by Heddon. The top of the line 3-30 with aluminum spool sold for $45 in 1920, to give one an idea of the value today (multiple of 10 at least). The book also shows the rods available

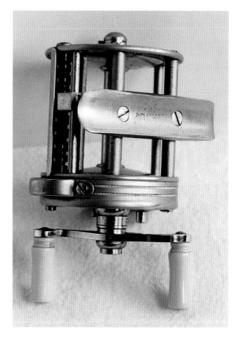

beginning as early as the 1910 catalog. I would add any Heddon reel to my collection that is in very good to excellent condition, regardless of the age, as they only tend to appreciate in value.

Heddon Model 3-35

with leather pouch.

$335+

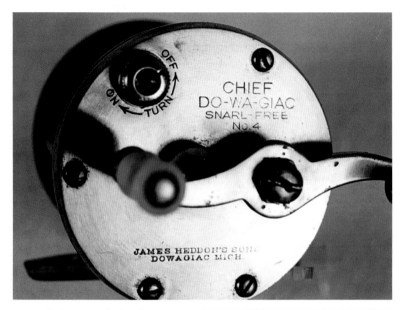

Heddon Chief Do-Wa-Giac

Snarl-Free No. 4, marked James Heddon's Sons.

$75+

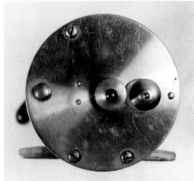

Heddon Model 57

automatic fly reel new in box with papers.

$125+

Heddon Model 57

well used.

$15-$20

Heddon Pal Model 41

level wind baitcasting reel.

$50-$75

Heddon Winona

steelhead type reel (Indiana style).

$100-$125

Heddon Model 45 baitcaster

with the early Carter's patents, marked James Heddon's Sons, also with thumb rest.

$300-$400

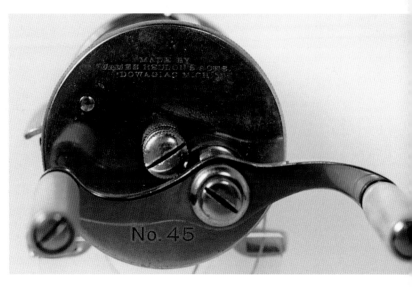

Heddon 3-15 baitcaster

in German silver, marked James Heddon's Sons, in original box with silk line.

$400+

Hendryx

Hendryx is one of the oldest of reel manufacturers, receiving its first patent for reels in 1887 and being in full production by 1888. By 1900, the company advertised it had already sold more than 2 million reels. The majority of the very early Hendryx reels were simple raised pillar reels, often without any click mechanism. However, the company also made some nice multipliers and hard rubber reels, including trout fly reels. The company was sold to Winchester in 1919 and then Winchester sold it to H-I in 1932. The early Hendryx reels all have four rivets on the foot, making them easy to spot. However, I have found a couple of foot patterns marked Hendryx that look more similar to a Montague or Pflueger foot. So beware, not all makers were 100 percent uniform in their designs. Once Hendryx was sold to Winchester, the foot style changed slightly and the yardage number on the foot became underlined. H-I continued this pattern. Hendryx stamped its name on many reels on the foot only. On the other end of the foot was stamped a number of patent dates, some for its bird cages and not only its reels. Although they are plentiful, the trick is to find reels in excellent or mint condition, and the boxes are nearly impossible to find. Also, the rare ones are the multipliers, and unusual handle types and hard rubber reels. I am certain we still have much to learn about this company that also made early metal baits stamped Hendryx. I have collected these reels for more than 10 years and still find many surprises, some of which are shown here. Values vary greatly, but are increasing as more people discover the multipliers and other better reels made by Hendryx. Many of the reels are found on ice fishing rods in the north, as they were a handy small size to mount on the rod. That is why many of them show up with two holes drilled in the foot for mounting to the wooden ice rod. Hendryx advertised heavily.

Rare Hendryx box

using the Sterling Pound for a trademark. This box would have held any number of reels shown in the 80-yard capacity in nickel plating. Notice that the Model No. 80 is the same as the yardage capacity.

$50+

Hendryx 60-yard multiplier

Note the four rivets in the foot and the foot design. Each rivet was really a pounded down portion of the single loop holding the foot onto the lower pillars, as can be seen in the photo looking down from the top of the reel. One can also see the Hendryx stamped on the left side of a photo on the foot and the patent dates stamped on the opposite side. The yardage is marked 60 on the center of the foot, but it is not underlined. If one finds an underlined version with this or a similar foot, it is likely a Winchester or H-I reel, depending on the styles.

$40-$60

Hendryx
80-yard
multiplier

nearly identical to details of the 60-yard multiplier.

$40-$60

Hendryx
40-yard
multiplier

with bone handle in nickel silver.

$40-$60

Hendryx
40-yard multiplier

with celluloid handle in nickel silver.

$40-$60

Hendryx
100-yard
multiplier

*with unusual and early "s"
shaped handle, but with
a slightly modified foot
(often done to fit reel seats).*

$80-$100

Hendryx 40-yard multiplier

with hard rubber gear plate cover and wooden handle.

$80-$100

Hendryx 40-yard multiplier

with wooden knob.

$40-$60

Hendryx raised pillar 40-yard

with wooden knob, very common type.

$30-$40

Hendryx 25-yard fly reel

hard rubber with wooden knob, no click. This is a very, very rare type of Hendryx and was found in an antique tackle box with another hard rubber reel. It is very small given the yardage. This has premium value even though it is missing one screw. Otherwise, it is fine.

$225+

Hendryx raised pillar 25-yard

with wooden knob, very common type, but not a common size.

$40-$60

Hendryx raised pillar 40-yard

with wooden knob, very common type, but with nice patina.

$30-$40

Hendryx raised pillar 60-yard

with wooden knob, very common type in rough shape.

$10-$20 in this shape

Hendryx raised pillar 100-yard

with wooden knob, very common type, but in excellent condition.

$40-$60

Hendryx multiplier

40-yard with bone knob.

$40-$60

Hendryx 40-yard multiplier

with double click, bone knob, marked on head plate "Hendryx" and with a reel foot similar to an early Pflueger. According to White, and others, this should not be, but it is. It may be that at one time Hendryx purchased reel feet from Pflueger, or may have copied the design for a period. I have three reels marked Hendryx with this configuration, so I know I am correct on it being a Hendryx. The main identification difference is that the ends of the foot are not as rounded as a Pflueger foot. It may be a later Winchester-made Hendryx as well, given the foot. See Winchester later.

$80-$100

Hendryx 40-yard multiplier

similar to the one shown two reels previously, but with the double-loop reel seat and an underlined yardage marker, bone handle and double click. Likely made right after the sale to Winchester in 1919.

$50-$75

Hendryx Model 4904

with 40-yard marking underlined, indicating Winchester-made (little tag is when I acquired it).

$100+

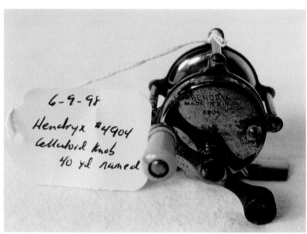

Hendryx multiplier

40-yard with wooden knob, hard rubber click, silk line and made of aluminum. This is a more unusual Hendryx reel to find.

$80-$100

Horrocks-Ibbotson (H-I)

Horrocks-Ibbotson of Utica, N.Y., was one of the largest tackle suppliers in America for a number of years, wholesaling the wares of others and manufacturing its own items as well. A number of myths about this historic company need to be put to rest. It is a very old company, making rods, lines and selling terminal tackle since as early as 1910, as the 1949 catalog is its 39th Edition. The catalog claims the company began in 1812 and I know that it was providing some components to the rod industry very early. I have archival materials from Halls Line Company corresponding with H-I in the 1800s. In 1949, its 39th catalog stated its address as Utica 2, New York, and its factories were located at both Utica and Rome in New York. It also had a sales office at 18 Warren Street, New York, N.Y. (as did one of its predecessor companies purchased in 1930, Abbey and Imbrie). It sold the very early auto fly reel Y & E, although it did not make the reel originally. It contracted with other major companies for rod making, such as Shakespeare, making some of this Kalamazoo, Mich., company's rods for them. It was sold to Gladding (the same as South Bend) in about 1960, and that is when lure production in wood ceased, as did the reel production. Some claim that at one time it was the largest of all makers of tackle, with more than 400 employees in Utica.

Because we know H-I purchased some lures from Arnold and rods from Shakespeare and others, it is likely that the company contracted for some reel production. The earliest reel that the company acquired the rights to is the Yawman & Erbe automatic fly reel, started in 1883 and purchased by H-I in 1911. It also appears some of the later reels were Bronson and Ocean City models.

According to Phil White, it acquired the fishing reels of Winchester in 1932. We need to sort out many things about H-I, both before and after its various acquisitions, but a few of its reels are shown here. One item I failed to photograph and should have is the fairly common Bakelite fly reel called the Vernley. It is an interesting shape with a number of squared off corners. It is an excellent functional reel. One may be seen at a number of Internet sites, including online auctions.

"Y & E" Auto

key version made until roughly 1930 by H-I. This is a very collectible early fly reel.

$125+

Old H-I advertising figure

on box for Model No. 1000 reel, no reel. These boxes with the fish designs are some of the most attractive available.

Box only, $10-$20

Bakelite casting reel

level wind with click, with very clean lines, trademark stamped on foot design similar to a Bronson.

$10-$15

H-I Admiral

No. 1840 with celluloid spacer and knobs, level wind nicely constructed and similar to many Bronson designs, with the extended adjustable drag similar to some Ocean City reels.

$45-$60

Ruby 80-yard multiplier

beautiful jewels, double-click mechanism, single counter-balanced crank with the Pflueger-type Hendryx foot identified earlier in that section with 80 underscored. This is either an H-I or a Winchester, in my opinion.

$200+, as it is unusual

Hurd

See the Hurd rod/reel combinations in Chapter One for details on these fine reels that were only made for a short period from the late 1940s to the early 1950s. They trade regularly in the $150-$250 range, depending on condition and if the rod and case are also excellent.

Jamison

Jamison Model "11"

open face spinning reel. This large supplier of fishing lures also supplied a few reels to our fishing history, including this very early spinning reel. This is a patent pending model of the unusual little reel. Note the protrusion on the reel seat shaft that acts as a means to kick the bail back into place after casting. Many early spinning reels used this design. The reel has components of steel, plastic and aluminum.

$25-$35

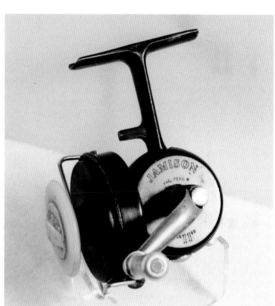

Japanese Reels

Although one was shown above under Great Lakes, many additional Japanese reels found their way to America in the 1950s and 1960s. Some of the reels were likely produced under contract (today we call it "outsourcing"), and some were mere knock-offs that hit the American market to compete with our own producers of reels. It was definitely one contributing factor to the demise of many of our major tackle producers in America. Many of the reels are unmarked as to model or number and only stamped with Japan, while others provide many interesting details. Most of the reels are low-end, but once in a while a very fine reel appears with the Japan imprint on it from the time period. This is not an exhaustive study of these reels, but it should give the reader one more thing to look for while building a collection.

Jupiter Model 300

level wind baitcaster. Most of the blue paint is worn off this inexpensive, but smooth-working reel.

$5-$10

Spin-High open face spinning reel

with shaft design similar to the Jamison Model "11" shown earlier. Drag is marked "drag" and Japan is on the reel seat.

$10-$20

Simple unmarked level wind

works great. Footplate is marked Japan and has a "6" in a little circle.

$10+

Trimline Model R-250

modernistic-looking level wind with single click.

$15-$25

Karmann Model No. 41

open face spinning reel similar to a Pflueger Pelican crossed with a Mitchell 300. This is a fantastic reel and it works like silk. Foot is stamped "Made in Japan."

$50+

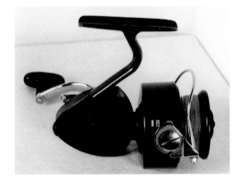

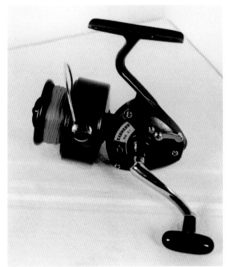

Another unmarked simple reel

stamped Japan on foot.

$5-$10

Olympic Model No. 35

fly reel in red. A beautiful little fly reel with clicker that has more details on foot than most: "Made in Tokyo, Japan, Ueno Pat.," clear plastic winding knob. This has the distinct appearance to a number of Ocean City models of the same time period (late 1950s-early 1960s).

$30-$50

Angler Rainbow

Model #72 fly reel with click. This is using an old venerable name and looks similar to a Pflueger Medalist. As a matter of fact, a very similar reel is shown in the Pflueger section, stamped with the Pflueger "P" and also stamped Japan, as is this one.

$30-$50

McCoy open face spinning reel

made in Japan. This interesting little reel is similar to many early European designs made in Japan with the great American name of McCoy.

$20-$30

J.C. Higgins

Sears Roebuck & Co. used the trademark of J.C. Higgins for many of its sporting goods, especially hunting and fishing items. It also used Ted Williams, as we saw earlier, and I will show a tackle box later with his imprint. The early J.C. Higgins items were made by most of the major tackle producers. It appears that Bronson, Ocean City, South Bend, Shakespeare and others provided reels for the name brand. During the 1960s, Sears outsourced some of its items to Japan, as the first two items shown demonstrate. The nice thing from a collecting point is that the prices on these items seem to maintain well, as more and more are specializing in a J.C. Higgins or Sears collection.

J.C. Higgins Model No. 3980

level wind baitcaster, used, in its Made in Japan box. Reel is marked J.C. Higgins on its head plate and is stamped Japan and 248-39800 on its foot. Bronson-type design.

$30-$40 boxed

J.C. Higgins Model No. 3112

level wind baitcaster, used without box. Foot is stamped opposite of the one above with the number on top, 248-31122, and Japan on the bottom. Head plate is marked Sears instead of J.C. Higgins. These two reels show the pitting often found on inexpensive reels of this era.

$20-$25

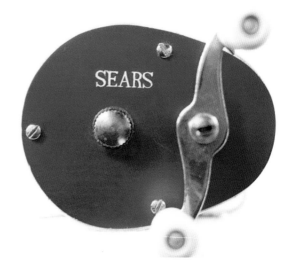

J.C. Higgins Model 3103

level wind with box and details. Bronson made this gorgeous reel for Sears and it has the most detailed engraving of any I have seen. Note the details of the game fish engraved onto the head and tail plates. Details of the box are shown, as well as some paperwork for the reel.

$100+

Model 3105 J.C. Higgins

level wind, stamped 537.31050 on head plate. One crank knob is missing. This is an older Bronson reel design.

$15-$20

Model No. 46 J.C. Higgins

level wind, stamped also No. 312.3104 on head plate above the model number; Bronson-made reel. One screw is missing; otherwise it is in very good shape.

$15-$20

J.C. Higgins Model 312.31130

fly reel with Medalist appearance.

$20

J.C. Higgins Model 311-3115

fly reel with a Meisselbach appearance, likely from after Bronson's acquisition of the company.

$25-$30

Johnson Reels

Johnson reels are as familiar to most anglers in America as Zebco reels. Denison-Johnson, Inc. of Mankato, Minn., manufactured the reels. Ranger Reels of Rockford, Mich., will be featured later in this chapter. An interesting development was the invention of a closed face-spinning reel by Ranger, sold to Johnson, that became a million seller. Sorry to say for Ranger, it stuck with the baitcasting line, which was slowly dying out after the war and right when it invented its reels. Due to their familiarity and postwar production, there has been less interest in these spinning and spincasting reels than others. However, there are some real sleepers and any of the Johnson reels in mint condition or new in the box should be collected.

Johnson Princess Model No. 100AP

This used reel is rare, as it was marketed only in 1954-55 for women anglers. Lionel corporation did a similar thing with the "Girl's Train" in pink and pastel colors in the late 1950s and it, too, is very rare and costly. Johnson marketed the 100AP in 1954-55 and the 100BP in 1964-65, both pink reels for women anglers. As with most gimmicks, it did not catch on well, as an angler is an angler regardless of one's sex at birth. However, these are very rare for Model 100s.

$50+

Johnson Princess Model No. 100AP

new in its box with all of the correct paperwork, box stamped 600124. Even the box and the instructions were in pink. The only flaw is where someone likely removed the price sticker from the top of the box when giving this as a gift. This is the only boxed one I have found in 10 years or more of looking.

$200+ in this condition

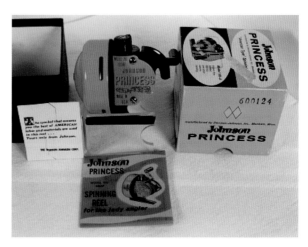

Johnson Century Model 100

This is well used, but the earlier version of the Century 100. Compare to the next reel.

$10-$15

Johnson Century Model 100B

This model is more recent, but new in the box, from the 1960s.

$30

Johnson Sa'Bra Model 130B

This larger model came with 400 feet of 15-pound test line already spooled, along with a casting weight and nice cloth bag for reel storage. This reel is harder to find than the Model 100s shown above.

$40+

Kalamazoo Tackle Co.

Nice can

for an American Boy Model 1706 level wind reel.

$10+ for can only

Kalamazoo Tackle Co. "Thrifty"

Model 7107 level wind reel.

$35+

Kopf Patent

Early reel history is a mass of confusion regarding patents, inventions, licensing and sorting out all of the variations in minor details. Reel expert Steven K. Vernon has done us all a great favor by researching these small nuances in his *Antique Fishing Reels*, 1985, published by Stackpole Books. He gives us great details on patent history and to whom the patents were sold, transferred or licensed. One of the patent dates always used to identify a reel as Kopf-type reel, but not necessarily a Kopf reel, is Nov. 24, 1885. His patent number 330,985 was for a corrugated reel foot that fit over the two pillars on the bottom of the reel and then was soldered into place. He apparently licensed this invention to a number of firms making reels with its design, including the Wm. Mills & Son reel makers.

An earlier patent dated Nov. 14, 1871, by Silas B. Terry of Waterbury, Conn. (number 121,020), also developed a new foot design obviating the need for any pillars or cross-bars on the bottom of the reel. The Terry design was a one-piece foot with

upturned flanges that attached directly to the head and end plates with screws or rivets. Terry assigned his patent rights to his own Terry Clock Co. and may or may not have also licensed it. I am including the Terry information here, as the two reel seats are similar and can be confused. The makers of the reels shown are not known with certainty, but the foot design we do know.

Kopf and Terry reels

shown in detail later.

Terry-type 40-yard brass fly reel

with built-in click device, marked foot, wooden lathe-turned crank knob in walnut. Foot is 2 5/8" long and the reel is only 1 15/16" outside dimensions. There is light corrosion where someone once placed a sticker on the foot. Shown also is a nice antique reel screwdriver next to the reel.

Reel, $150+; screwdriver, $5-$10

Brass 1 1/2" reel

with 1 7/8" reel foot soldered to solid flat cross bar instead of lower pillars, bone or horn handle in "s" shape without counter-balance. The reel is extremely smooth and very well made. This may be the nicest reel in my collection for workmanship and smoothness, given its age. This reel may also be an English import from the early 1800s. If it is a Conroy, it is from about 1850.

$500+

Kopf 100-yard fly reel

in brass, yardage marked and patent mark on foot, no other markings. Note that, other than the foot differences, it is constructed identically to the Terry reel shown first in this section. The final close up details the patent date and the soldering technique on the foot.

$100-$125

Kopf 40-yard fly reel

in brass, yardage marked and patent mark on foot, no other markings. It is next to a Meisselbach Featherlight No. 250 with a diameter of about 1 3/4". Similar construction to the other models, but with two holes drilled for attachment to an ice rod.

$100-$125

Langley Corp. Reels

As already shown in Chapter One, Langley produced collectible rods and also made a number of excellent reels for fishing and collecting. I had one manufacturer's representative tell me that he believed they were the smoothest of all major commercially available level wind reels. And he was buying antique tackle and not selling me anything. I do know that most of mine still run very smoothly.

Box for Model 410

"Whitecap" level wind baitcasting reel.

$10+ for box only

Some bags

for Langley baitcasters.

$5-$10 each

Langley Streamlite

Model 310 with date code of KB. The open spool design is typical on many Langley reels.

$25-$35

Langley Lakecast

Model 350 on left and Streamlite Model 310 on right.

$25-$35 each

Langley Reelcast

Model 500, showing details. Foot says Made in U.S.A., Pat. Pending, as it does on all the others shown.

$40+

Lawson Machine Works

Laurentian No. 1, dry fly reel

by Lawson Machine Works, Montreal, Canada.

$20

Marc
Marc "Hoosier" style reel

very unusual and quite scarce.

$100+

Martin Auto Fish Reel Co.

The name says it all for this reel manufacturer located in Mohawk, N.Y. It was an early and prolific producer of automatic fly reels. There are no less than 20 varieties with its own name, plus some made for other companies. Patent dates include 1892, 1895, 1903 and 1923, and many reels are so marked. Also, many simply say "Patent Applied For," but they are not always the earliest ones, so be aware. Early boxes are hard to find and the reels are often well used and worn in appearance. They almost always remain very smooth functionally. I feel these are underrated in pricing. I recently sold a very early box, papers and reel for less than $60 online, far less than its historical value given the difficulty of finding the boxes. The automatic reels in general do not command much money, likely because most think they are "modern." Not all are new, with many being from the late 1800s or early 1900s. One finds this trend true with Shakespeare, South Bend and other auto fly reels as well.

Martin No. 2

1923 patent, natural metal color, brass drag adjustment.

$20+

Martin No. 28

"Pat. Appl'd For" model.

$20+

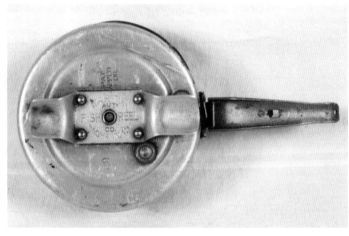

Martin No. 2

"Pat. Appl'd For" model, brass drag adjustment, black model.

$20+

Martin No. 8

Patent No. 2176756 model, black and aluminum.

$20+

Martin No. 8A

Mohawk model in blue.

$20-$30

Meek Reels

We have stepped up our collecting a few notches above the rest now. Meek reels were some of the original Kentucky-style reels originally made by B.F. Meek & Sons and then sold to Horton Manufacturing of Bristol, Conn., in 1916. Once produced by Horton, all of the reels were machined whereas they were hand-built in Kentucky. However, many feel that the quality of the Horton-Meek reels is as good or better than the originals. Some of the more common reels include the Blue Grass 33 and the Meek #3. Any of the tournament reels are scarce, as are some of the reels made under contract for others. The company was the source of Bristol rods beginning in the 1880s. It produced both rods and reels from 1916 until its demise right after the war in the 1940s.

The smoothness of a Meek cannot be appreciated from the photos. To understand the demand for these reels, one must hold one, feel the smooth movement and see how the reel exudes quality from all components. This is also true of the better Meisselbach reels and the Vom Hofe reels, among others. But the German silver Meek reels are about as nice as any I have ever manipulated. They are not impossible to find, but are rare and are difficult to find in the field. Once in a while one gets lucky, as I did finding the Meek #4 on an old rod in a garage sale, but that is very rare indeed. Recently I did buy two Meek reels from a field find, but paid a fair price for them. The boxes are far scarcer than the reels and are a wonderful find for any collection. My recent field find included two boxes and bags with original excellent condition reels.

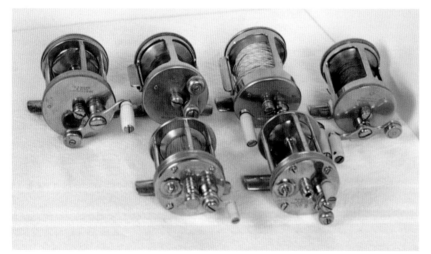

Meek, Blue Grass and Heddon Carter patent reels

Details of the Heddon reel were shown earlier and the others follow.

Horton/Meek Blue Grass #3

Serial No. 14223, found in excellent condition in a box with the bag. Can you imagine my excitement to open a box and find this treasure inside? It was one of five vintage reels from a recent field find.

$500+

B.F. Meek & Sons Blue Grass No. 33

made by Meek in Kentucky. Reel foot is stamped with the number "1" and there is no Carter patent on the reel, indicating it is prior to 1904.

$300+

B. F. Meek & Sons Blue Grass No. 33

made by Meek in Kentucky. Reel foot is stamped with the number "4" and Carter patents are present, meaning post-1905 reel.

$300+

B. F. Meek & Sons Blue Grass No. 25

with Carter patents and reel foot stamped number "2," made in Kentucky.

$350+

B.F. Meek & Sons Blue Grass No. 33

with Carter patents and "3" stamped on reel foot.

$300+

B.F. Meek & Sons Blue Grass No. 33

with rare first Carter patent only and Patent Pending stamping. So this reel is a 1904 or 1905 reel for certain. This reel was found with its silk line in place.

$400-$600

B.F. Meek & Sons No. 2

serial number 3198, made in Kentucky, with a beautiful patina and smooth as silk. One sold in 2001 for $1,576.

$2,000+

Meek/Horton No. 2 Tournament

with narrow spool and balsa arbor, serial number 11157, in gorgeous patina and perfect mechanical condition. This is a hard reel to find in the Tournament size.

$1,000+

Neptune German silver Model 53

60-yard multiplier with beautiful patina in original box and bag. Phil White attributes this name to Montague, but this appears to be a Meek or Talbot click design. Regardless if a Meek, Montague or Talbot, it is a gorgeous reel from the turn of the century era not often seen in a box. It is one of the very rare reels made for Wm. Frankfurth Hardware Co. of Milwaukee in the early 1900s, using the Neptune brand name. According to author, and Wisconsin expert, Bob Slade, all Neptune brand products are worth a premium over similar products due to rarity.

$1,000+

Meisselbach Reels

Another fine company with a varied history, ending up under the Bronson banner eventually, is this old company that began in New Jersey in 1885. I cannot do any better than the excellent work done by Phil White on these reels and the company history. So I would visit **www.oldreels.com** or buy his book on Meisselbach reels to study and learn more about these excellent products. The early Expert, Featherlight trout reel, trolling reels, and Tripart and Takapart reels are all in demand, as are the Symploreel types. One of the fun parts of collecting these reels is to collect all of the name stamping differences as the company moved, changed owners and added partners. A Meisselbach in excellent condition is a nice find and an excellent addition to any collection of reels.

Meisselbach Tripart and Takapart reels

with a Simmons Special Tripart in between them. The two on the left end are Model 580 Triparts and the two on the right side are Model 480 Takaparts and the one in the center is the Simmons Special Tripart. Foot markings include the A.F. Meisselbach & Bro. Newark, New Jersey and the A.F. Meisselbach Mfg. Co. Elyria, Ohio marks. Simmons Special is the rarest.

$50-$100 each

Tripart 580

made in New Jersey by A.F. Meisselbach & Bro.

$50-$75

Symploreel No. 252

Level winder, double crank, made in Ohio.

$100+

Meisselbach Model 270

Featherlight skeletal fly reel with click, counter-balance weight mounted on the spool front and a wooden crank knob. Featherlight stamped on front near foot and No. 270 stamped on foot bottom.

$75-$125

Meisselbach Featherlight

Model 250, no city or maker markings, black wooden knob, counter-balance weight on the spool, stamping on top of the reel. This is a diminutive reel as shown under Kopf listings.

$60-$90

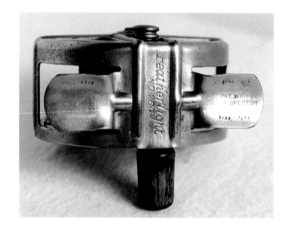

Meisselbach Featherlight

Model 260, stamped A.F. Meisselbach & Bro. Newark N.J. on top of the reel. Foot also has patent stamping on foot ends.

$60-$90

Expert large skeletal fly reel

by Meisselbach, two versions. Both have the three patents from 1886-1889.

$150+ each

A.F. Meisselbach Mfg. Co.

No. 100 Level Winding Reel made in Ohio is Bakelite. This simple reel is quite attractive. Many of the Meisselbach Bakelite reels are nice additions to a collection, if in fine shape.

$15-$25

Two early and unmarked trolling reels

likely Meisselbach. The second one has the anti-backlash spring that is likely a Meisselbach. Both reels have had a counter-balance weight or knob removed from the spool front for some reason.

$100+ each

Mitchell Reels

Briefly discussed under Abu earlier, Mitchell spinning reels were among the first major and the most successful American imports. The Mitchell began in France and many service personnel returned home with the "new fangled" design for light fishing. Many brought along a rod and some tackle too. Some spinning items had been advertised in the 1940s, but by 1947 Airex and Mitchell were already making inroads into traditional baitcasting and fly-fishing markets. Spinning is far easier to master than either of the other two forms of casting and is only beaten for ease by spincasting. It is also versatile, allowing one to use a small clear bobber and use flies and other light tackle. I grew up a baitcaster due to the tradition of my neighbor/mentor Nick; however, most baby boomers rapidly adopted the new techniques of spinning and spincasting, and many folks 45 or younger in America have never used anything else for fishing.

This is not going to be an in-depth treatment of all the minor variations of the Mitchell reels, as I am only half-done and already running out of space. But this will at least alert the collectors to yet another reel to ponder while looking for new additions to their collections. For all of the details to make even the most demanding historian happy, go to **http://users.skynet.be/mitchell-collectors.org/** and read for hours.

The Frank Borman reel

given to him by Garcia Mitchell for Apollo 8, as discussed earlier. This reel is not for sale. It is a Garcia Mitchell Model 408 designed for ultra light spinning.

$150+ new in box for Model 408

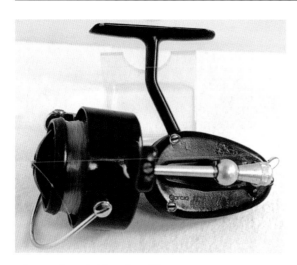

Garcia-Mitchell 300

made in France, paint has been retouched, three-prong drag type.

$25 as it is retouched and rough

Mitchell

without number, indications made in France, serial number 235892.

$75-$125 in this condition

Original Mitchell wooden line spool

front and back, from France.

$10+

Unmarked Mitchell

and some related collectibles, line spool from Garcia and spare spools with line from Mitchell.

Reel, $50; other items, $5-$15 each

Unmarked Mitchell 300

from 1950s, large saltwater Model 486 and a Japanese import called McCoy shown earlier in this chapter.

McCoy, $20-$30; early Mitchell, $30-$40; Mitchell 486, $100+

Montague Reels

This major rod and reel maker acquired the patents of other companies such as Malleson, Conroy and the U.S. Net & Twine Co. in or about 1899 to begin making reels. It had been making rods since 1892 and bought Chubb in 1891. A foot patent originally assigned to the U.S. Net & Twine Company later became a Montague style. Eventually Ocean City purchased the company and, in 1934, started making the reels although rods continued to be made at the Montague factory. In 1955, the name was changed to the Montague-Ocean City Rod & Reel Co. Montague history is about as confusing as identifying its reels. Montague made reels for a number of jobbers and wholesalers, and even for other reel makers such as Vom Hofe. Thanks to the work done by Phil White and others, we now know the names of a number of the generic reels produced by Montague.

This is a company that is severely underrated as to values, especially for its hard rubber trout reels. They are every bit as nice as a Pflueger Delite or a Leonard, in my opinion, but sold for a fraction of those until recently. I think others are also noticing the quality and the demand is increasing now, as it should. At first blush, it is nearly impossible to tell apart the hard rubber/German silver reels of Montague from those of Pflueger or Vom Hofe. Montague also made a number of Kentucky-style reels that are beautiful and still affordable. The company also had many raised pillar designs, from the inexpensive to the more complex. I selected Montague to collect more than 10 years ago, as the reels were affordable and just as high in quality as most. Apparently others have now joined my selection, as prices are on the increase for better Montague reels. To learn more about the company history or to see a list of generic names produced by Montague click on **www.oldreels.com** and visit Phil White's informative Web site on reels.

Foot comparison

of a Montague on left and Pflueger on right. As with the Hendryx reels, the simple way to identify a Montague raised pillar reel is by its foot if it is not marked by name. Other than the slight variation in the counter-balance weight design, these two reels are identical in design except for the foot. A Montague raised pillar reel foot is rounded with four little "ears" bent up, through which the lower pillars are inserted. Note there is spacing between the "ears" and the plates. Yardage is stamped on the foot bottom without underlining. The foot ends on the Montague are squared similar to a Hendryx foot. Now note the Pflueger on the right. The foot ends are gently rounded. There is also spacing between the foot edges and the plates, but the foot is indented in the area where the pillars are inserted and the foot is raised between the pillars with the yardage stamp marked without underlining. After seeing a few in this book or handling a few, it is easy to tell them apart. However, as seen with the Hendryx reels earlier, there may be unknown variations and many foot patents were licensed by major makers. So one might find a variation that is still a Montague.

$40 each

Montague Climax 80-yard multiplier

with double click and beautiful knob. Both Montague and Pflueger used the hatching around the plates.

$40

Montague Climax 60-yard

dent in one rivet and handle has a slight bend.

$40

Montague Indian 40-yard

$40+

Montague Badger Kentucky-style reel

crank knob has a slight bend and there is scratching to head and tail plates, 60-yard capacity.

$75-$125

Montague St. Claire 60-yard

$50+

Montague photo essay

of fine hard rubber/German silver models from left to right: Pennell trademark made for Tryon Company, 60-yard model. Free Spool is a Montague brand for one of its saltwater reels, 100-yard model. The V. L. & A. is one of its casting reels, 100-yard model. The photos go from left to right and each reel is then detailed separately from the Pennell, to the Free Spool to the V. L. & A. being the last one. These are exceptional reels and beautiful to hold and use. They are all very smooth. Note the Free Spool has the Julius Vom Hofe type star washer on its pivot. Ten years ago these silver/hard rubber Montague reels sold for $100-$150 and now they should be valued at three times that amount given their quality.

$300-$450 each

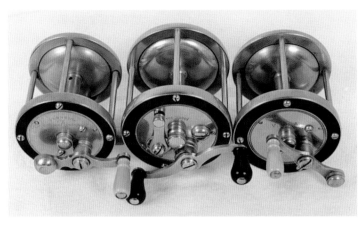

Montague Huron Kentucky-style reel

60-yard model. Huron is a known fly reel for Montague, but White does not have it listed for this type.

$100-$150

Montague Professional multiplier type reel

60-yard model. Note the stamping of "Steel Pivots" appearing on many Montague styles.

$75+

Montague Premier Kentucky-style casting reel

60-yard model. This is the prettiest of the Kentucky styles that I have seen and is likely named Premier due to its construction and materials used.

$300+

Montague simple raised pillar reel

40-yard, no markings at all.

$20+

Montague quadruple multiplier reel

wooden knob, 60-yard, foot stamped.

$40

Montague quadruple multiplier reel

wooden knob, 60-yard, foot marked and reel slightly bent.

$20+

Montague Louisville casting reel

Kentucky-style reel, 60-yard, foot marked, works beautifully and is very smooth.

$300+

Montague unmarked hard rubber

150-yard double-click trolling or ocean reel.

$150+

Montague Pacific Surf Casting

saltwater reel, 150-yard, hard rubber/German silver. Note the foot is identical to the tiny brass reel shown under Kopf, attributed as a possible Conroy. This may be an example of Montague using one of the other foot types it purchased in 1899.

$300-$450, depending on condition

Montague 80-yard

unmarked hard rubber/ silver baitcaster, non-level wind.

$200+

Montague Trout fly reel

100-yard hard rubber/nickled silver fly reel. Trout is a model name stamped into the top of the head plate about 1/2" under the center screw, not visible in the photo but it is to the naked eye. This one is in kind of rough shape. It was found at a farm auction.

$150-$300, depending on condition

Two more Montague fly reels

both 40-yards, one is jeweled, both fine shape.

$300+ each

Ocean City Mfg. Co.

It is funny that Ocean City follows Montague naturally in this book, as the company eventually purchased Montague, circa 1934. There also seems to be some relationship between Bronson and Ocean City regarding the level wind baitcasting reels, but I have not figured it all out. However, I have shown some reels that are surely Bronson designs if not Bronson made. I also have at least a dozen Bronson-type reels with no markings that may be Ocean City. The main difference is the extended drag adjustment, with most other components being identical. Even the footplate with the two holes is identical. My research on lures has shown that a lot of sub-contracting was done for painting and assembly between the large companies, and this may be an example of that type of relationship. However, with all the interest in reels today, I am certain the facts will be eventually documented regarding this relationship.

Ocean City produced a number of large saltwater reels originally, thus the name Ocean City. Eventually it added a number of other reel types. Some of its modern fly reels are beautiful, even the inexpensive single action models. The baitcasting reels were likewise fairly common standard types, with many offerings of inexpensive pressed steel/plastic combination reels. However, one thing I have noted about the inexpensive newer reels is how smooth they tend to be. So the materials were inexpensive (and often corrode), but the workmanship was excellent. Since the company was located in Philadelphia, it is also likely that many of the early Ocean City reels were contracted for manufacture with neighboring makers in New Jersey, New York and elsewhere. We will learn more about this company as more collectors are drawn to it for its relationship with Montague and as more concentrate on the modern era of 1940 to the present. Plastics were being developed and used by Heddon and others, and there were so many economic changes and sales of companies that it nearly resembles what happened in the early 1980s.

Ocean City Fortescue

German silver, 250-yard ocean reel. This reel has jeweled end caps, a large wooden knob and the one-piece foot is marked 250. Note the Vom Hofe-type star on the palm side of the pivot.

$100+

Ocean City Bay City model

Bakelite, 250-yard ocean reel. It is very similar to a Pflueger model shown later. Also note the two-hole foot similar to the latest Bronson foot pattern.

$50+

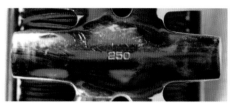

Ocean City Model No. 1581

level wind baitcaster, 100-yard model, used in box, circa early 1960s. This inexpensive reel works well, but shows some of the common corrosion. Many of the reels simply had stamped metal parts. The plastic stays perfect on these reels, but the metal is often pitted if not stored in a dry environment.

$10-$30, depending on condition

Ocean City Model No. 998

level wind baitcaster, double crank. Click is missing, but reel is excellent otherwise and was found in the wrong box. Note Bronson design similarities.

$10-$25

Ocean City Nile model

level wind baitcaster, double crank, jeweled end caps and better construction than most of the reels of this type.

$35-$60, depending on if boxed

Two Ocean City Model 970 reels

Note the small differences in these two reels, especially on the style of the head plate gear cover. The first one has a crank nut replaced.

$15-$25 each

Ocean City Model 88 Smoothkast

level wind baitcasting reel. This is an inexpensive but smooth working reel, circa early 1960s. Note the foot is exactly the same as on the Bronson reels of the same time period.

$10-$15

Penn Reels

It makes not only alphabetical sense for Penn to follow Ocean City, but the two companies were both located in Philadelphia, and both concentrated on saltwater reel production and sales. As with many companies, an employee of one left and started a new company, thinking he could build a better reel. Otto Henze migrated to America from Germany in 1922 and began working as a machinist for Ocean City reels. He left Ocean City to begin his own company in 1932, calling it Penn Fishing Tackle Manufacturing Company. His first sales were in 1933 and the company was off to a good start. He decided early on to name his reels after seaside communities to help promote the fact that he concentrated on reels for the surf and ocean anglers. The Henze family remained an integral part of the company, and Otto's spouse and son were active in its management and growth. In January 2003, the company was sold and the Henze family no longer maintained a management role. Herbert Henze had been operating the company since taking over from Martha in 1963, until the sale of the company to Jerry Rodstein. All of the historical details and photos of the very first Penn reel designs are found at **www.pennreels.com** for your viewing.

Penn Model 85

with leather thumb drag.

$40-$60

Pre-ZIP boxes

for two Penn reels, circa 1950s.

$10-$20 per box

Penn Long Beach Model 60

new in the box with original tissue wrap, catalog and wrench. Last pre-ZIP box type. The Long Beach was one of the first three reels developed by Otto Henze, which he originally called his Model K. Penn introduced the Penn Spinfisher reels you see advertised in the catalog in 1961. So this reel must be from 1962-1963, being pre-ZIP. I recently found three of these reels from an estate in California, where all the fishing tackle had been stored since the early 1960s.

$75-$100 new in box

Penn Long Beach Model 65

excellent, in wrong box. This has the fancy decorations molded into the head and end plates.

$50-$75; box $20

Penn Model 155

found in wrong box with reel lubricant tubes and wrench. The orange tube is the older one and it originally came in a two-piece box inside the cardboard case. Also shown is the reel mounting device for securing the reels from the bottom.

Tubes, $5-$10 each; reel mount, $2-$5; reel, $40-$60

Perrine

Perrine Free Stripping Model 50

automatic fly reel, black. This is the one patent and patent pending version. This was made in Minneapolis, Minn. These are excellent but newer reels, and I found a case of them from the 1960s recently. They all sold for $60-$80 each, new in the box. There are both vertical and horizontal mount versions, as with many fly reels.

$30-$40

Pflueger (Enterprise Manufacturing Co.)

Did you think we would ever get to this old manufacturer of reels? Of all of the big six lure companies, this is without doubt the oldest and the one that produced many fine collectible baits and reels since the 1800s. The company produced reels under its own name, the name Four Brothers and an inexpensive line often stamped Portage. Shakespeare purchased Pflueger in 1966, just two years after Pflueger celebrated its 100th anniversary as a tackle company. By 1966, neither Shakespeare nor Pflueger were doing much with lures, but were both concentrating on rod and reel production, for Pflueger reels especially.

The Pflueger Supreme is one of the most successful of all fishing reels in history. It was never cheap, but was always in demand due to its quality. It had an impact on reel history from its inception in the 1920s until the 1960s. The reel had the same impact on fishing in America and now reel collecting as the Abu Ambassadeur, it was just 30 years sooner. In two of my earlier books, I reproduced, with the permission of Shakespeare/Pflueger, complete catalogs showing all of the many dozens of reels produced by Pflueger (and Shakespeare) for many different years.

It is impossible to fully cover Pflueger reels in a brief section, but I shall try. A sampling only can be given, as there are so many models and variations. The Pflueger reels are in three general historical classes as I see it: (1) early raised pillar models similar to Hendryx and Montague reels from the late 1800s; (2) hard rubber/German silver or nickled silver combination reels such as the Delite models shown from the early 1900s; (3) the baitcasting revolution, beginning with the Supreme. Pflueger also made skeletal fly reels and the famous Medalist line of fly reels. Eventually it added the Pelican spinning reel and some others, but never really cornered the spinning or spincasting market, as Shakespeare did. I have only bought one new casting reel in my life and it was a Pflueger Akron. I have only bought one new fly reel in my life and it was a Pflueger Medalist. I still have them both and they are in perfect working order nearly 40 years later. Need I say more about the value of these reels?

Pflueger Ajax raised pillar reel

80-yard, double click, wooden knob.

$50-$75

Pflueger 80-yard unmarked raised pillar

Ivoryoid knob, double click.

$40-$60

Pflueger 60-yard unmarked raised pillar

Bakelite knob and double click.

$40-$60

Pflueger 60-yard unmarked multiplier

bone knob.

$40-$60

Pflueger Portage trademark Sentrie reel

It is nearly identical to the previous reel except with a Portage name.

$40-$60

Pflueger unmarked 60-yard raised pillar

Ivoryoid handle.

$40-$60

Pflueger hard rubber raised pillar

80-yard, Bakelite knob.

$100+

Climax 60-yard multiplier

White attributes this to Montague and Lawson lists it by itself. The foot does not appear to be Montague to me and is not exactly like a Pflueger, either. But I think it is more Pflueger than Montague, so I put it here. It is a gorgeous little reel regardless and was selling for $100+ more than 10 years ago.

$100+

Photo essay

of two Delite fly reels and an unknown reel. Some of the most outstanding early Pflueger products are the Four Brothers hard rubber and silver reels. One photo shows a Delite on each end and an unknown in the center that I do not believe to be a Montague. It could be any one of a number of fine fly reel makers. But the foot differences are easily seen between the two Pflueger products and it.

$350-$500 each

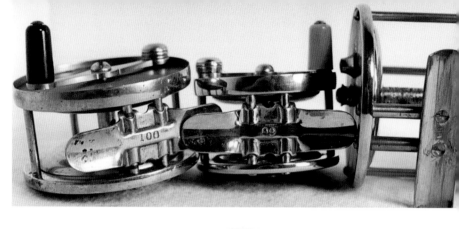

Four Brothers Capitol

100-yard casting reel and the two Delite fly reels from the previous entry. Note the Capitol is jeweled. One photo shows the palm side compared to one of the fly reels.

$150+

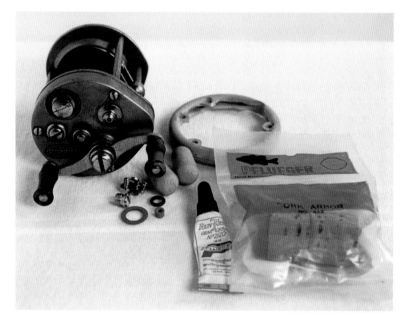

Pflueger Supreme No. 1576

and some goodies. These, and the earlier Supreme models, are the reels that secured Pflueger a name in fishing reel history forever. Not that the reels shown earlier did not help, as they did and they were also great reels. But with the invention and/or improvements of the level winding system, the Supreme became the supreme reel in the 1930s through the early 1950s, until the Ambassadeur started competing with the Supreme. There are many, many variations of the Supreme and only a few are shown.

$50-$75

Two modern box types

for the Supreme.

$10+ each

Pflueger Supreme

with Cub handle. The reel is satin finish shown with the last box type for the Supreme from Pflueger. The plastic presentation box is chipped, but it is lined with red velvet-type material.

$50-$75

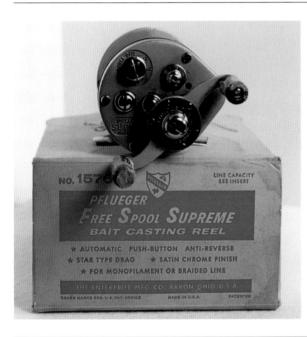

Reel bag

for a Supreme from the box with the blue modern P logo.

$2-$5

Early Model 1573 Supreme

the 1926 patent date version, with cork arbor. This early model does not have any patent data on the foot, only on the palm side end plate (tail plate). The foot has been slightly filed as can be seen in the photos, with it being squared off some for a reel seat. The reel works perfectly, as though it is brand new. The reel is jeweled on its one end plate. The crank side says "Pflueger Supreme Reg. U.S. Pat. Off." Level Wind Anti-Back-Lash. The reel has a lot of surface marring, but is sound and is as found in a tackle box.

$125-$150

Pflueger Model 1573 Supreme

1941 version. This has the Pflueger name embossed on the side and the foot says Patented Pat's Pend. Close-ups show all the details including the 1940s-50s multicolored line we used to land the big ones at Clear Lake in the 1950s.

$40-$60

Pflueger Model 1573 Supreme

1941 version. This one shows a close-up of the Cub handle, rubber palm ring and the leather bag with the Bulldog trademark.

$40-$60

Older Pflueger box types

for a Model 1993-L Summit and a Model 1963 Nobby, and some of the paperwork with the reels. One Summit is shown. In my opinion, this is the prettiest of all Pflueger reels. Even though it is merely a machined engraving, it is beautiful.

Boxes, $20+ with hang tags; Summit reel, $40-$60

Pflueger Akron

with box.

Box, $20+; reel, $30-$40

Pflueger Nobby

examples.

$30-$40

Pflueger Summit

$40-$60

Pflueger Medalist 1495DA

with leather bag. This is the modern version of the famous line of Medalist fly reels. These are simply great reels. They function wonderfully and are also finely crafted.

$40-$60

Pflueger Progress No. 1774 fly reel

This is a more inexpensive model than the Medalist, but it also worked well. It does not hold its paint as well as the Medalist.

$30-$40

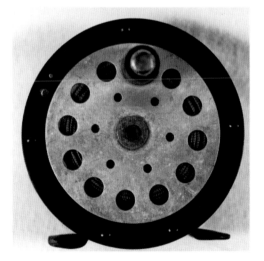

Progress No. 1774

slightly different.

$30-$40

Vintage Pflueger Progress

60-yard skeletal fly reel. This gorgeous brass reel with a wooden crank knob has a beautiful patina and works great.

$150-$175

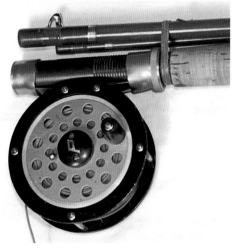

Pflueger fly reel

made in Japan, with the three-piece Fenwick fly rod shown in Chapter One.

$20

Pflueger Model No. 1558

Sal-Trout heavy trolling reel. This is not the inexpensive Sal-Trout model fly reel Pflueger also made. This is a well-constructed and beautiful trolling reel.

$50-$75

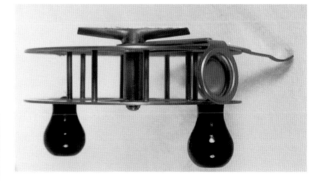

Pflueger Taxie

Model 3126 heavy trolling reel with the early Meisselbach-style side drag. The rim is also marked "B" near the model markings and has two nice large wooden knobs for retrieve.

$40-$60

Pflueger Oceanic

*free spool, surf casting reel.
German silver/hard rubber,
bulldog trademark and leather
thumb brake/drag.*

$100+

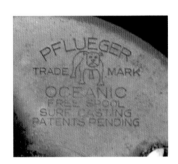

Pflueger Norka

*Model 1335 saltwater reel. The line
guide is slightly bent out of shape.*

$40-$60

Pflueger Model 1978 Ohio

and similar Pflueger Golden West Model 1878 saltwater reels in Bakelite with large wooden knobs.

$40-$50 each

Pflueger Bond

saltwater reel, Model 2000.

$30-$45

Precisionbilt (Aerco)

This gorgeous reel is one of only a couple built by this Hollydale, Calif., company.
It is a translucent maroon that the photos do not due justice for its beautiful color.

Precisionbilt MAR-100

*patent pending model of the Marquette
baitcasting reel.*

$50-$60

Ranger Reels

This Rockford, Mich., reel company of the late 1940s-early 1960s was located in the town where I have had a law practice for a number of years. I was fortunate enough to interview both family members and former employees. It has a similar story to Hurd reels. The effort was put into developing a beautiful baitcasting reel at the wrong time in history, just when spinning was taking over. The sad thing for Ranger is that it also developed two spinning reels that it did not produce in any numbers. The company made the further mistake of selling the rights for one to Johnson, which became the Johnson Model 10. When I first wrote about the company, I did not think (and neither did my sources) that the spinning reel was ever put in production, but at least one has been found new in the box so a few must be out there. The baitcasters are well made, and were developed after extensive research and commentary by anglers.

Rare Ranger reel display

full of Heddon Punkinseed next to a Ranger "Grand Prize" model baitcaster shown later.

$250+

Ranger Grand Prize baitcaster

$25+

Ranger Grand Prize

with cork arbor in green.

$20-$25

Ranger prototype

spinning reel purchased from the family.

No established value, archival piece

Record

An early Swiss invasion of spinning reels was from this company. They are fairly hard to find in excellent condition and very nice to add to a collection.

Record spinning reel

Swiss-made, with original paperwork.

$50+

Shakespeare Company

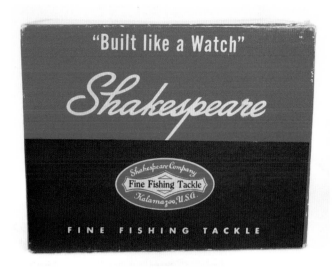

A book could be, and needs to be, written about Shakespeare. This wonderful old tackle company is one of the big six, according to all writers, and is definitely one of the big two in reel production, along with Pflueger. Of course, Shakespeare later bought Pflueger so all the reel production among lure makers was really concentrated in one company, with only South Bend providing any significant competition after 1966, and then not much. To cover only Shakespeare reels would take a huge volume and the 100-plus photos shown here are only a beginning. However, it is a start and will give the reader a good idea of the wide variety of Shakespeare items to collect.

Box types

for Shakespeare reels.

$10-$20 each

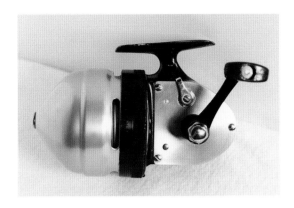

Shakespeare Model 1810

Spin Wondereel, new in box, with papers and wrench, Model DK (1971). This is one of the finest spinning reels ever made and I have sold numerous versions (older ones are in more demand due to stainless steel bearings) for more than $100 each.

$125+ boxed

Shakespeare Model 1770

Wondereel, early type of spinning/casting reel by Shakespeare, Model FD (1957).

$25-$35

Shakespeare Model 002

from the recent era.

$10+

Shakespeare Hoosier model

Indiana-style reel found in garage sale with a South Bend rod.

$100+

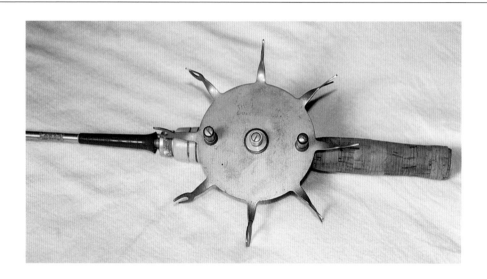

Shakespeare Kazoo

skeletal fly reel found on a bamboo rod at garage sale.

$40-$60

Shakespeare Kazoo

fly reel, a second example.

$40-$60

Shakespeare Russell

fly reel, small size, Model 1894.

$30-$40

Shakespeare Russell

fly reel, larger size, Model 1896, GE (1946).

$40-$50

Shakespeare Russell

fly reel, Model 1884, GA (1940).

$30-$40

Modern Shakespeare

fly reel imports, Model Alpha 2528G.

$5-$10

Shakespeare Model 1821

"OK Automatic" fly reel, excellent, in box with papers.

$30 in box

Shakespeare Model 1837

Tru-Art automatic fly reels. One on the left is Model GD from 1947.

$25+ each

Shakespeare Model 2226

Ocean Prince saltwater reel with Bakelite end plates.

$75-$100

Shakespeare Model 2222

Ocean Prince. Model HD on the foot indicates it is from 1937.

$50-$75

Early Shakespeare

(1922 Model) baitcaster with hard rubber gear covering and early dial drag mechanism.

$50-$75

Shakespeare Ideal

No. 1963 Level-Winding reel.

$30-$40

Shakespeare Professional

Model 1924, No. 23053, early high-end baitcaster with jeweled end caps, dial drag, hard rubber gear cover.

$85+

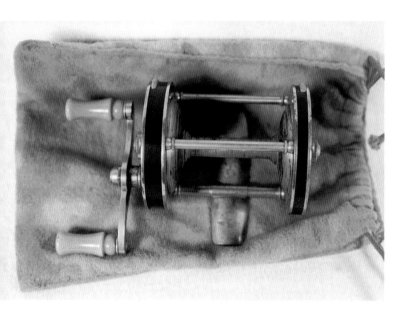

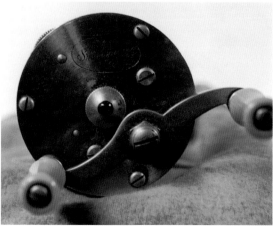

Shakespeare Precision reel

three versions, shown in detail next.

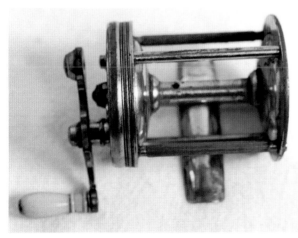

Early Shakespeare Precision

Model 25401, 1912 model, and foot is still marked "W.S.JR.CO." on the bottom.

$40-$60

Earlier box

for the Universal Model 1063.

$30-$40 for box only

Universal Precision

by Shakespeare, Model 1745 HE, meaning from 1936.

$50-$60

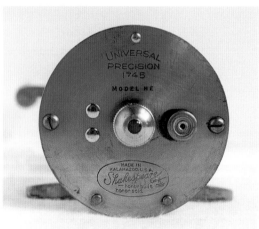

An earlier Precision

No. 23041 with jeweled end caps and single counter-balanced crank.

$50-$60

Earlier Universal Precision Shakespeare

Model 23041 with jeweled end caps and double crank.

$50-$60

Wondereel

the reel that made Shakespeare famous, No. 1921 GK from 1941 shown next to a later spool box for a Wondereel spinning reel extra spool.

$20+

Shakespeare Wondereel

Model No. 1921 GE from 1946, a great find, excellent in a can with bag and papers.

$75+

Top-notch Shakespeare

Model 1922 Wondereel DeLuxe in Nickel Silver, Model HB from 1939. This is a very fancy Wondereel with nice knobs and gear covering.

$25-$30

Box and reel details

for a Shakespeare Tru-Blue Model 1956 from 1951 (Model FK).

$40 boxed

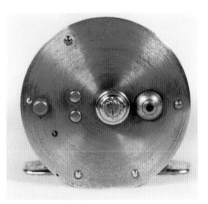

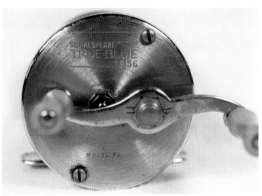

Earlier box

from 1946 with an excellent Shakespeare Criterion Deluxe, Model 1960 reel, jeweled end caps, fancy knobs, with bag. Model GE indicates made in 1946.

$50+ boxed

Two Shakespeare Criterion reels

from 1946 (both Model GE).

$30+ each

Direct Drive Shakespeare

Model 1924 with box. FK reel makes it a 1951 version. Wexford line is advertised on the box.

$20-$25

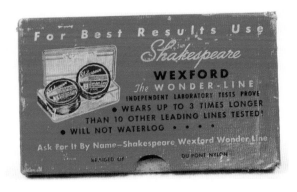

Model 1950

Direct Drive Shakespeare.

$15-$20

Criterion

older version by Shakespeare. Non-jeweled, end plate says Criterion Level Winding No. 1960 and foot says the 1924 model.

$35+

Shakespeare Leader

No. 1909 from 1957 as seen by the "FD" on the end plate.

$20-$30

Shakespeare Acme

Model 1907 with Bakelite gear cover.

$20-$30

Another famous Shakespeare

the Marhoff type in nickel silver made in 1946 as seen by the "GE" on the end plate. The Marhoff patent was one of the firsts of the William Shakespeare Jr. Company acquisitions that allowed the company to edge out most other reel producers in the early 1900s.

$25-$35

Direct-O-Drive

*Model 1950 Shakespeare with jeweled
end caps and large star drag.*

$30-$40

Shakespeare Imperial

*Model 1957 1/2, made in
1940 as indicated by "GA"
on head plate.*

$20-$30

Shakespeare DeLuxe Wondereel

Model 1925 made in 1940 (GA code) only in stainless steel now. This is a beautiful reel that does not deteriorate with age, as some do. Note the fancy scrollwork on the foot pillars.

$50-$75

Shakespeare Triumph

Model 1958 made in 1946, right after the war.

$15-$20

Unmarked Shakespeare

made for Sears (World's Largest Store).

$30-$40

Shakespeare Model 1937

Direct-O-Drive "Free Spool" version made in 1963 (code EH on faceplate) similar to a Bronson Invader and the one shown earlier with the Ted Williams rod.

$75+

Various Shakespeare items

related to reels: small parts tube, extra spool and an early box for spin/cast reel.

$5-$10 each

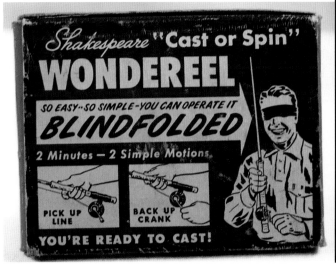

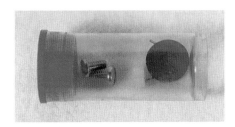

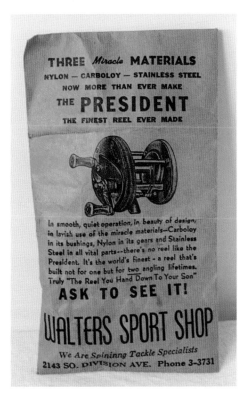

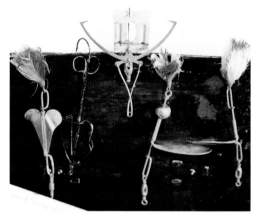

Transitional essay to South Bend

This photo essay shows an early Shakespeare tackle box (painted) and an early Marhoff reel by Shakespeare on the left and a Model 1131-A South Bend on the right. The Marhoff says on the foot it is the 1918 model. The South Bend has the 1905 and 1906 patent dates and is serial number 13456A. The lures shown include many South Bend early lures, an early CCBC Pikie, a brass stringer and a very rare Haas Brothers (Benton Harbor, Mich.) ball bait and spinner, among others. This tackle box was one of my best "field finds" ever and credit goes to my wife, Wendy, for finding it for me. Out of it came the Rhode's Frog, new in cardboard box, that sold at Lang's a few years back for $4,000 and a few other pretty good baits.

Reels: Marhoff, $75+; South Bend, $75+; box, $50+; lures, $20-$200 for most

South Bend Bait Co.

A book could be written just on South Bend reels. South Bend is still in business, but now only as an importer of items. It no longer makes the Oreno line of lures, which is now owned by Luhr Jensen. South Bend originally sold to Gladding Line Company, then to Glen L. Evans of Idaho and then to Luhr Jensen. The early 1960s sale to Gladding fairly well ended the collectible era of South Bend reels. South Bend made early baitcasting reels and competed heavily with Shakespeare, making spinning and spincasting reels in the 1940s-1950s. There are numerous small model differences with South Bend reels. Collectors will often search hard and long for a "letter" model they do not have, such as an A, B, C or D version of some common numbered reel. South Bend, as Bronson, Shakespeare and Pflueger, made reels for other distributors, so one will often find an unmarked South Bend made for a jobber or catalog retailer. South Bend was first to exploit the early anti-backlash dual-bar system and likely bought the patent from its developer. Many of the early reels have serial numbers, making them even more interesting to collect.

A typical South Bend box

This one was for a Model 1000 seen later. The South Bend reels are shown in order of number, as most of them were known by the company by their model numbers and not names.

$10-$20 for boxes

South Bend No. 20

Model A.

$15-$20

South Bend No. 50

South Bend on foot.

$35-$50

South Bend No. 60

foot marked same as Model 20.

$15-$20

South Bend No. 300

Model D.

$20-$25

South Bend No. 350

Model C.

$20-$25

South Bend No. 550A

$20-$25

South Bend No. 790

"Smoothcast Direct Drive."

$20-$25

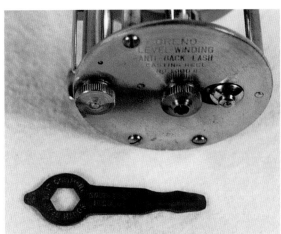

Reel, box and wrench

for a Model 1000 Oreno Model B. This has the double bar anti-backlash device, as found on all early South Bend reels, and also has nice jeweled end caps.

$50+ boxed

ORENO
No. 1000 B
LEVEL WINDING
ANTI-BACK-LASH
CASTING
REEL

Unmarked South Bend 1000

made for another company that is marked Sure Stop LW ABL (for Level Wind, Anti-Backlash), as marked on many South Bend reels.

$25-$30

South Bend Model 1000 G

$25-$30

South Bend Oreno
Model 1000

without letter designation.

$15-$25

South Bend Oreno
Model 1000 B

$20-$25

South Bend Model 1131 A

serial number 11599, with the 1905 and 1906 patent dates.

$75+

South Bend Model 1131 A

with single crank knob and counter-balanced handle, jeweled end caps.

$75+

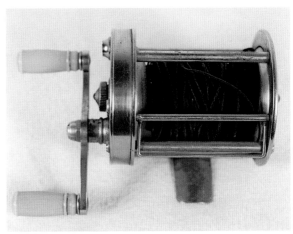

South Bend Model 1131 A

serial number 40216 A. Early patent dates are also on foot. Jeweled end caps with double crank knobs.

$75+

Futura spincasting reel

futuristic looking, from the 1960s, Model 101.

$20-$25

South Bend Finalist fly reel

modeled after the Pflueger 1494 series of reels.

$25-$35

Modern Chinese imported reel

South Bend 1122A fly reel.

$15-$20

South Bend Oren-O-Matic

No. 1140 Model D automatic fly reel.

$20-$25

Two Weber Futurist fly reels

flanking the South Bend No. 1151 made for South Bend by Weber.

$50-$75 each

South Bend No. 1151

fly reel made by Weber (a Futurist).

$75+, as South Bend is rarer

Staro Reel

Staro Serial No. 29141 spinning reel

another Swiss import very similar to the Record shown earlier.

$50-$75

Union Hardware Co.

This is the same company that made the metal rods shown in Chapter One. The two most common reels are the Sunnybrook raised pillar, that nearly always is missing paint from the wooden knob, and the skeletal fly reel in any number of versions, many made for other distributors. The rare one is the Samson, shown later, with the neat opening head plate showing the gears. It is kept together by a simple pin depressed to open the plate and gear mechanism. This early invention was to prevent losing parts on the take apart-type reels. Also rare are boxed items such as the Model No. 7225 quadruple multiplying reel.

Union No. 7225

S level winding reel, excellent in box.
This is a rare find in the box.

$50+ boxed

Samson reel

showing all of the details of this interesting opening reel.

$60-$75

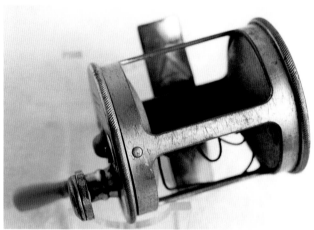

Union Sunnybrook

raised pillar with painted wooden knob. Two versions, plus a third foot is shown to show how many are found on ice fishing rods.

$25+ each if excellent

Three Union fly reels

details, open skeletal type. First one in brass is marked, the other two are stamped Made in U.S.A.

Brass, $30-$40; others, $20-$25 each

Vom Hofe Reels

For most collectors, including me, it just does not get any better than this. The Vom Hofe brothers, Edward and Julius, descended from a reel-making father, took over his craft and expanded upon it. Edward made superb saltwater reels and rare trout fishing fly reels. Julius made numerous types of reels and was more prolific. Either maker is extremely collectible and, overall, the reels by Edward are more valuable. However, the small Julius reels are coming of age with collectors and are a wise investment. These late 1800s and early 1900s makers are as fine craftsmen as we have seen. They are on a par to the Meek/Horton reels, but of a different variety due to the age and the training of the makers. In addition to reels, Edward allowed his name to be on one very collectible spoon and there were also Vom Hofe tackle boxes. The reels shown are a good sampling of what to expect if collecting these beautiful reels.

Two small Julius

and a large Edward Vom Hofe reel on the right. Details shown later.

Model 621

6/0 Edward Vom Hofe saltwater reel in superb condition. Both end caps have maker's name and patent date of May 20, '02 (1902) stamped on them.

$450-$600

Early Montague reel

marked German silver that was sold by Edward Vom Hofe & Co. of New York and is so marked on the reel handle. Many makers made reels for others to sell and Montague jobbed reels out to many makers, even famous ones such as the Vom Hofe brothers.

$300+

Julius Vom Hofe

beautiful little brass raised pillar multiplier, with his trademarked hole in the foot center. Not all Julius reels have this hole, but it is present on most of his designs. It is a sure sign of one of his reels. This is a Model 3 1/2, with his other trademark seen on the palm side end plate, the eight-star pivot washer. The patent date is Oct. 8, '89.

$200+

Julius Vom Hofe

Model 3 1/2 with hard rubber gear cover and end plate.

$150-$200

"Brook" jeweled fly reel

and Julius Vom Hofe hard rubber fly reel. The Brook does not have a center hole, but otherwise looks like a Julius Vom Hofe. Phil White attributes it to Montague. The small hard rubber one is a Julius Vom Hofe for certain and was found in what I believe is a Vom Hofe tackle box shown later.

$300+ each

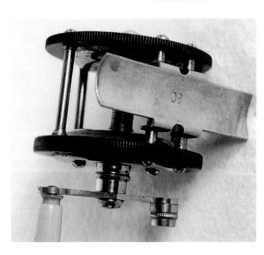

Two Julius Vom Hofe reels

one made for V.L. & A. of Chicago (early sporting goods distribution house). Details later.

Julius Vom Hofe

showing the nice star washers and both patent dates as previous.

$250+

V.L. & A. reel

head plate showing details and two patent dates of Nov. 17, 1895, and Oct. 8, 1899.

$250+

Two reels

compared further. The foot of the V.L. & A. is marked "1" and the other is marked "4."

$250+ each

Julius Vom Hofe

with the Pennell trademark for Edw. Tryon Co., compared to a similar Montague.

Vom Hofe, $200+; Montague, $100+

Model 3 1/2

details (stamped on foot) Vom Hofe Pennell reel showing both patent dates, star washers, the star pivot washer with two lobes broken and the hole in foot.

Alligator model casting reel

by unknown maker: likely a Montague, but the quality of a Vom Hofe. Foot is stamped "60" and the end plate is stamped "Steel Pivot Bearing" as are many Montague reels.

$100+

Hard rubber "60" reel

near perfect, maker unknown but it is either Julius Vom Hofe or Hendryx. This was found in a little antique shop in Wisconsin's Northwoods along with a Philipson rod.

$300+ as is

Montague V.L. & A.

German silver saltwater reel. It is shown here to compare with the other V.L. & A. and with Vom Hofe reels in general. This is a large 250-yard model with beautiful jeweled end caps. Note the Steel Pivot Bearing markings.

$150+

Weber of Stevens Point

I have written more about Weber than anyone and own the archives of most of the historical data, purchased from the company's former president a few years ago. The company with collectible reels is known as "The Weber Lifelike Fly Co., Stevens Point, Wis." This is the trademark we are most interested in finding. However, Weber Tackle did continue to market some of the reels under its later trademark as well. Everyone has a favorite, but to me it is hard to top the Futurist as also shown under South Bend. It is so "modernistic."

Futurist fly reel

Weber Model 300 in correct web design box. The box is harder to find than the reel.

$125-$150 boxed, early box

No. 300
WEBER
Futurist
FLY REEL

"Silent Knight" fly reel

Weber Model No. 500. This one is very sturdy and well made, and is quite hard to locate.

$60-$80

"Weberkraft" nylon fly reel

Weber Model No. 500. The company recycled the number from the Silent Knight reel for one of the nylon reels. This is new in the box with all details and paperwork, including the extra pawl. Also note that the company dates back to 1896, the time of Carrie Frost's company.

$50-$75 boxed

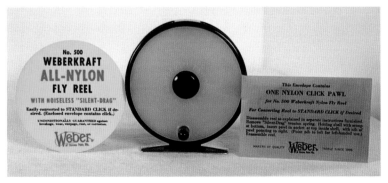

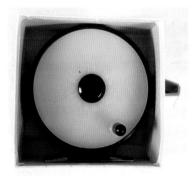

Weber Weberkraft fly reel

in gray nylon, new in the box.

$50

Unknown reel

likely made for Weber. The name Waterwitch has been attributed to a Montague fly reel, but it was also the brand name for early Frost products. This may be a reel made by Montague for either Carrie Frost or G.W. Frost, predecessors of Weber.

$40+

Winchester (formerly Hendryx)

Winchester is one of the most collectible names in antique and collectible circles. One competes with collectors from all fields for Winchester products due to the company's popularity. Last year I sold an oil can for $450 (utility can) and have sold many lures for three figures. Even metal Winchester lures are collected. Most metal lures do not bring much, yet these sell for $50-$100 with regularity. Winchester reels have an interesting history, first made by Hendryx and then being sold to Horrocks-Ibbotson. Many Winchester reels are unmarked and one simply needs to look for a Hendryx-type reel with the yardage marking now underlined on the foot. Also, as Phil White points out, the foot is sometimes slightly different. The marked Winchester reels command the most money. There is an interesting and little-known fact among collectors: the little wooden knob, inexpensively pressed steel reels are often Winchester reels. I was fortunate enough to find a new one in its box and the box is identical to the Winchester fly reel box. Many other companies also distributed these little stamped reels, but now we may be able to identify one for certain.

Winchester Model 4253

80-yard reel.

$175-$200

Basscaster 80-yard reel

with Pflueger-type raised foot, but with underlined marking similar to Winchester after it took over Hendryx. I think it is a Winchester.

$50-$75

Model 2230

raised pillar Winchester reel with bone knob, marked by model and company, 60-yard model with underlining. Note the foot is identical on the Basscaster.

$100-$125

Two Winchester reels

new in the boxes. Model 4400 Arrow Jr. Fishing Reel, single action, nickel plated with two wooden knobs, 80 yards. Also, a Winchester Single Action fly reel Model 1235 in a Model 1600S box, 60 yards. Bronson later made the Arrow Jr. reel.

Arrow Jr., $40+ boxed; fly reel, $125-$150

Back and foot

of Model 1235 Winchester fly reel.

$125-$150

Winchester fly reel

early brass, with no markings.

$150+

Tail plate and front

of Arrow Jr. on its box.

$40+ boxed

A second Arrow Jr. reel.

$25-$30

A third Arrow Jr. reel.

$25-$30

Wright & McGill

"Colorado-style" reel

early version, by Wright & McGill called the Fre-Line, no patent numbers or model number on the back. These types of reels were side-winding spinning types that were unique to the Rockies.

$25-$35

Fre-Line

later model, with patent numbers and Model 10BC found on the back, along with company name and Denver, Colo. U.S.A.

$30-$40

Yale

Yale German silver fly reel

in larger size.

$200+

Unmarked Yale

or Yale-type early fly reel with wooden knob.

$125+

Smaller Yale

German silver fly reel with wooden knob.

$200+

Carlton fly reel

shown to compare, similar to Yale and from roughly the same time period (1903-1908 for Carlton).

$150+

Zebco

Well, we end the chapter with a "Z." Most people who think of Zebco think of the modern inexpensive plastic reels that every kid uses at one time. However, Zebco is a fine company and makes fine reels. It was one of the very first companies to introduce us to "closed-face" spinning or spincasting reels, circa 1950. The company got its name from the Zero Hour Bomb Company of World War II. The Model 11s shown under the rod chapter are excellent and they are beautiful early reels. Many of the early 1950s and 1960s models are very collectible and a few are hard to find. I cannot show all of the varieties here, due to space and our concentration on more classic reels, but I am showing a couple that deserve to be on any reel collector's shelf, including the Model 11s shown earlier.

Model 11

foot shown in the rod chapter.

$40-$50

Zebco box

is my all-time favorite. It is the Zebco Model 202 Zee Bee reel made for ease of casting for kids and others.

$30-$40 boxed

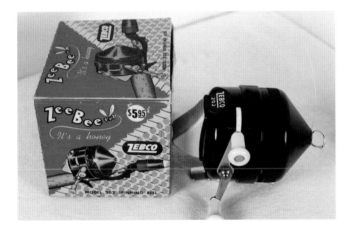

Another classic Zebco box

for a Model 44 underslung spinning reel. Note that the cost was $19.50, making this 1950s reel fairly pricey and not the inexpensive reel many individuals believe the Zebco line to be, at least not during its first 10 years or so.

$30-$40 boxed; box alone, $5-$10

Modern Zebco 202 versions

$10 each

Chapter Three:
CREELS

Beautiful splint basket/creel

16" long, 10" wide and 6" high, with two splint latches and carrying handle. This basket may have been a boat/canoe creel or simply a nice basket for fish or picnicking. This is on display in my den and is surrounded by a few other fishing collectibles. The wooden case is a Montague Rod & Reel Co. display case for ferrules and rod silk. The little green book to its left was a gift to O.L. Weber of Weber fame. The reels have been seen earlier in this book.

$200-$300

I do not pretend any special expertise on creels other than to know their collectibility. They are also another example of a crossover collectible, with many home decorators and basket collectors competing for fishing creels or baskets. Creels have been made of various materials, but the two most common are rattan and willow, either split or whole. In Michigan, we also encounter Native American fish baskets made of birch bark. There are specialty books on creels available. Likely the best source for pricing creels is to follow the Lang's auctions and get the actual sales prices for creels sold at auction. It is not unusual for Lawrence, Macmonies, Simeonov and Turtle creels to command $1,500 or more, if in excellent condition. The high sale known was a Simeonov from 1930 selling for $3,050 in 1999. Turtles hover around $500 and many Lawrence creels bring $1,500-plus, with recent sales exceeding $2,000 each.

Most fish baskets or creels were first designed for trout fishing, or at least for stream fishing. An angler would simply place the creel over his shoulder and then have an instant carrying device for the fish until they hit the frying pan. Many creels will still have their "shoulder harness" on them and that should increase the value overall. Nearly any creel will sell for more than $50 and some of the great leather-adorned, brand name creels command easily more than $1,500 in many sales. This is a huge variation, so how does one tell? Well, most creels came to America from Japan or British Hong Kong. Some were imported from France. Many were leathered after they were brought to America. Artisans specializing in creel making in America handcrafted some. And quite a few are American, made by either local craftsmen or Native Americans. The name-brand creels are the ones with the most value. These are normally marked in some way. Japanese creels are at the low end and most British Hong Kong creels are moderately priced due to the added leather. French weave creels are a little more. Native-made creels vary widely in pricing. Most of the 50-plus creels that I have owned have sold for $75-$125, with a couple of exceptional versions bringing more than $200. I have never owned a "name" creel and have never sold a creel for more than $200, but I know many better creels easily reach the four-figure mark.

One general rule to note is that when the hole (through which to drop the trout) is in the center of the lid, it is normally an older creel. Creels came in a number of shapes and sizes, and some were even made for children. Repairs made to the creel will harm its value, whether they are repaired caning or new leather hinges. Many, many fraudulent creels exist on the market, so beware! This is one area where Caveat emptor is extra important. It takes little to "age" a creel and many unscrupulous sellers have done just that, so be careful and buy only from a reputable dealer. Many creels made in the 1960s are indeed collectible, but one needs to understand that creels were still available in the 1970s from Cabela's and other wholesalers that were not much different from earlier versions of creels.

As to value, they should start at $50 and go up from there. I sell most of the Hong Kong creels with leather trim and a harness for $150+, or $125+ without the harness. Creels have not gone up much in the last 10 years because they were already fairly high priced, often bringing $100+ at farm auctions as early as 1995. I sold two Japanese creels at auction for $125+.

Large whole reed creel

with carved wooden peg lid latch, center hole and leather hinges. Note the heavy weaving of the bottom of the creel for strength. The harness shown with it is not original. This is in excellent condition and is fairly unusual. I paid $200 in 1997.

$200+

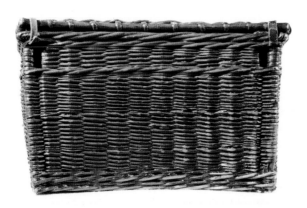

Japanese-type creel

with the fish-shaped leather hinge. It's my favorite. Most of these hinges are found with the "tail" below the metal clasp broken off or torn. This is a wicker creel with the hole on the side and all leather is original, with only minor edge wear on the side of the top.

$150+

Wicker Japanese fish hinge creel

with the tail broken. This harness may be original to the creel. The creel is actually a little nicer than the previous one except the tail is gone.

$150+

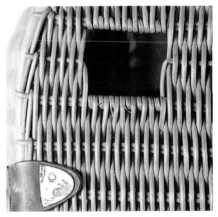

British Hong Kong creel

whole willow and leather trimmed. For those who cannot afford a Lawrence, this one has a similar appearance, but was made for the mass market. This is 9" across the top and the back of the leather has ruled markings for measuring the trout. Tooled harness is not original with the creel.

$225+

Small, 7" British Hong Kong creel

whole willow and leather trimmed, shown with some other fly fishing collectibles.

$200+ for creel, $10-$50 for other items.

Small, 7" British Hong Kong creel

wicker construction with leather trim, in excellent condition.

$200+

Wicker creel

with leather latch strap, stamped metal base on strap. Side hole variety, leather hinged, rough shape on lid. Origin is most likely Japanese.

$75-$125

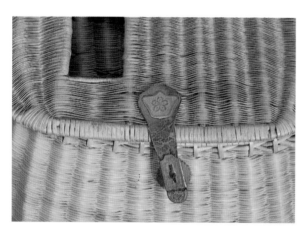 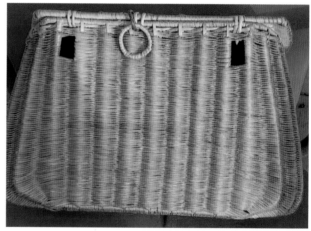

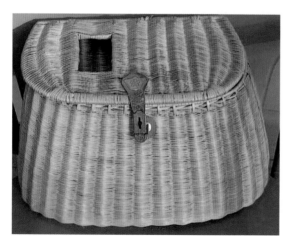

Split willow Japanese creel

with same latch type as previous creel. This creel is in excellent condition and dates from the 1940s or 1950s.

$150+

Split willow Japanese creel

with nice tight weave split willow and leather trim, long type of side hole, simple latch, wide leather harness is not original to the creel. Also shown is a rare little (2 1/2") fly reel made in 1884 in England out of Ebonite.

Reel, $300+; creel, $250+

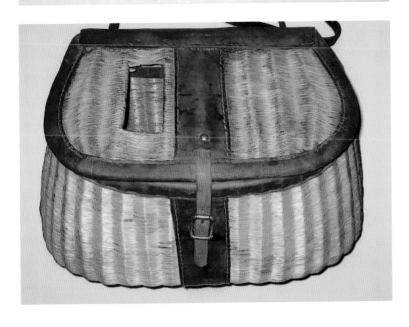

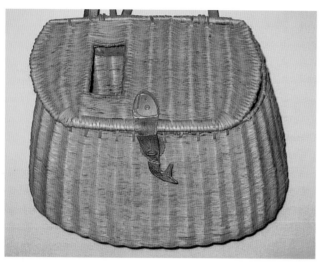

Nice Japanese split willow

with fish latch in excellent condition.

$200+

Japanese split willow creel

finely made, with older leather harness and a beautiful fish latch. Also note the small leather rosette under the fish hinge that surrounds the latch mechanism.

$225+

Japanese split willow creel

green tinted, with nice leather trim and a simple latch, side hole. Often this trim was added in the U.S.

$300+

French weave

or Japanese split willow with leather trim similar to previous creel. It is shown with my Hardy line dryer shown elsewhere.

Creel, $300+; line dryer, $200+

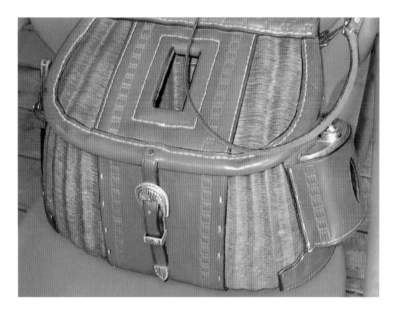

Creel

made by the great-grandson of George Lawrence, using the original tooling and techniques developed by his grandfather. W.C. Lawrence III is now in his 70s. Original Lawrences are selling for $1,500-$2,200 at this time.

$1,500

Lawrence-made creel

dated 8-11-99 with a nice bird pattern, full leather top, front fly wallet pocket, and 12" rule sewn in at back of top, similar to the Hong Kong creels shown earlier. This one is hand crafted and beautiful.

$1,500

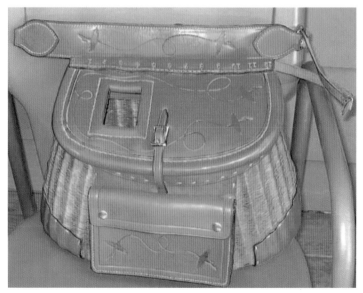

W.C. Lawrence III creel

made in his grandfather's style with front fly pocket, side knife holder, half-leather top, stamping on harness and beautiful split willow weaving.

$1,500

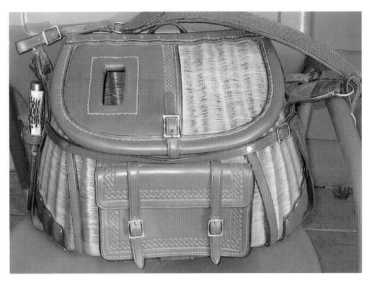

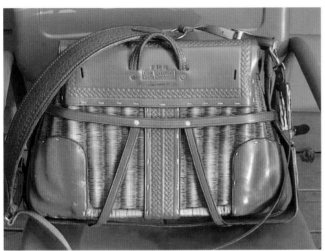

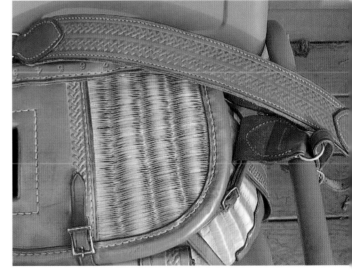

W.C. Lawrence III creel

made in grandfather's style in 1999. This one has a tooled leather top (about 60 percent), a side knife holder, an intricate narrow leather harness system and beautiful leather trimming all around. The tooling is a nice crosshatch basket weave to match the fish basket.

$1,500

Simple wicker creel

*with peg and leather latch system.
Braided hinges, wooden framed top,
nicely made.*

$150+

Huge whole reed creel

atop of a center-hole boat/canoe creel with legs. The creel has an intricate weave pattern front/center and a hanging loop on the rear. The bottom of the creel is reinforced with a double reed weave pattern and the top has a decorative weave pattern as well. The latch is a wooden peg into a braided reed. The leather boat strap is similar to one that just appeared in Lang's auction and may be original to these creels.

Creel, $400+; boat/canoe creel, $200+

Large splint creel

with center hole and designs; small child's basket/creel and modern creel. Details and values are given on each later.

Beautiful splint creel

with reed interweave design on top, bottom and middle. Interesting shape, with concave back, half-round front.

$400-$600

Contemporary

Native American child's creel.

$100+

Whole reed child's creel

with intricate woven front and handle.

$200+

French weave split willow

with leather top and trim, and a couple of nice fly wallets and related items.

$300+

Japanese split willow

with leather trim and some wooden nets that are collectible. The wooden nets from A&F and Cummings are very desirable and sell for $100+ with ease.

$250+

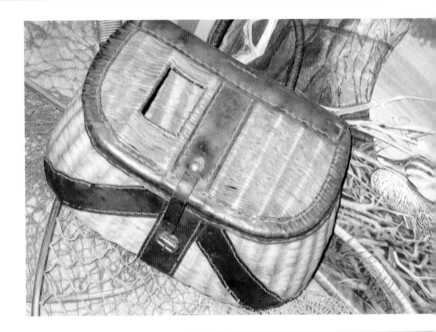

Wooden creel

folk art, 7 3/4" high, 10" wide, 5" deep, made of old crate slats and cedar.

$100+

Chapter Four:
BUCKETS, TRAPS AND BOXES

This chapter covers the growing area of collecting minnow buckets, minnow traps, bait boxes and tackle boxes. Most of these items in the past were seen as $5-$10 items at auctions and garage sales. Actually, many of the tackle boxes found are not even worth that, due to weight and difficulty of shipping. However, many early boxes are collectible and the field of minnow bucket collecting is rapidly coming of age as well. Minnow traps have been long valued and I cannot remember an Orvis selling for less than $100 in the past 10 years. Traps by Shakespeare and others will command hundreds of dollars. Other interesting containers include cricket cages and many other types of bait containers now being collected.

There is no "standard reference" at this time to these items and maybe this chapter will serve as a benchmark for collectors interested in these more functional items of fishing. One thing is certain, the days of the $5 minnow bucket or cricket cage are rapidly dwindling as folks recognize the value of these items. But keep in mind that not all tackle boxes are worth collecting and sometimes the best value is found in keeping them for storage, not posterity. Yet, a good UMCO, Kennedy, Heddon, Outing, Falls City, Union or Shakespeare box is certainly something with intrinsic value worth collecting.

River model

bait box details.

$25-$35

Clipper heated minnow bucket

made by E.L. Walstedt & Co., Minneapolis, Minn. A similar bucket was shown in a recent Lang's auction and it was stated it was the first one seen by that author. I have seen three others.

$100+

Minnow Buckets, Traps and Bait Containers

Not all anglers use lures and baits. Instead, many anglers use live minnows for their prey. Numerous inventions have come along over the years to trap minnows and then to keep them alive after being trapped. This is a growing area of interest to collectors, and little has been written on the subject. It is with great thanks to Terry McBurney of Ada, Mich., for his generous contribution of photos and captions for many of the buckets shown here. Without his assistance, this book would not have the breadth of minnow buckets shown. I also would like to thank the others named in the photo captions.

In addition to minnow traps and buckets, live bait was also contained in any number of interesting bait boxes and contraptions. A few of those are also shown. Again, little has been written on these items and they all used to trade for $5-10 each. As we learn more, the older and more unusual ones are commanding the value they deserve.

Lucky Floater minnow bucket

without the decal.

$100-$150

Grouping of minnow buckets

showing The Clipper and a Lucky Floater, Green River, Stay Alive, Flambeau and Falls City. Also shown is a small river model minnow bucket and three common bait boxes.

Buckets, $30-$150 each; boxes, $10+ each

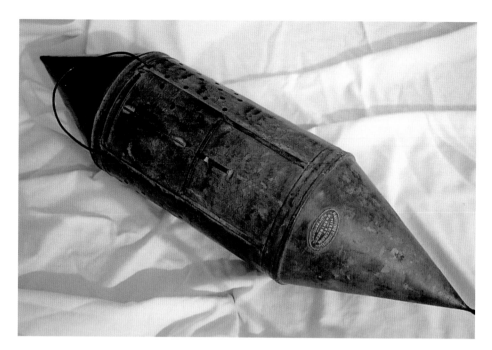

Shinners Minnow Keeper

$800-$900

William Shinners Minnow Keeper

very old and rare, and newer Frabill Minnow Bucket. The very rare "Hartford Minnow Float" is not often traded. It brings $800-$900 if it has the original plated-brass nameplate with the Wm. Shinners name and the Dec. 19, 1905, patent date.

Shinners, $800+; Frabill, $20

River model

minnow bucket, small and unmarked.

$25+

Frabill "Long-Life"

with star air hole design and unmarked galvanized bucket with minnow air hole mechanism installed.

$20+ each

Frabill Fullflote

pre-ZIP code, wooden handle.

$25+

Hall's Telescopic Floating Minnow Buckets

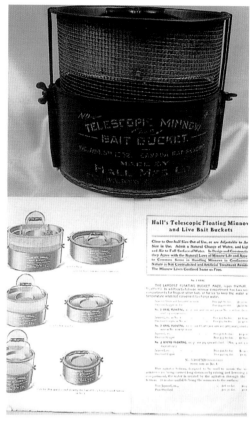

(Hall Manufacturing Co., Cleveland, Ohio). Hall was one of the earliest U.S. minnow bucket manufacturers. Its telescopic minnow bucket was patented on Aug. 5, 1902, so production most likely started in 1900 or 1901. It was the only minnow bucket recommended in Dr. James Henshall's classic Book of the Black Bass. This innovative minnow bucket cleverly telescoped when two wing nuts were loosened and the inner pail was pulled upwards. Hall made five different styles of buckets and offered them in two finishes. They were available in a green japanned finish or in oxidized copper. Value in very good condition would be $300 and up in the japanned finish. If you were lucky and found the copper version, the price would more than double. (Randy Spagnoli Collection)

$300+

Cream City #110 "Climax" 10-quart Round Floating Minnow Bucket

(Geuder, Pasachke & Frey Co., Milwaukee, Wis.) Cream City was the largest minnow bucket manufacturer of their time from early 1900 to approximately 1920. As one of the larger steel products makers in the U.S., it not only made minnow buckets and tackle boxes, but hundreds of "Cream City" products for the home and the farm, including oil and gas cans, garbage cans, water pails, fire buckets, galvanized pails, watering cans, wash tubs and boilers, milk cans, roasters, enamelware of all kinds plus many other items. There were three sizes in its Climax series: 8-quart, 10-quart and 12-quart. All were in a rich green japanned finish with gold bands and gold and silver lettering. (Randy Spagnoli Collection)

$200-$300

Cream City "Champion" Galvanized Oval 20-quart Non-floating Minnow Bucket

(Geuder, Pasachke & Frey Co. of Milwaukee, Wis., approximately 1916-1920) Cream City also made minnow buckets for the Shakespeare Co., and Shakespeare's #770 1/2 "Classic" oval 20-quart non-floating minnow bucket is identical to the Cream City "Champion." (Terry McBurney photo)

$50-$100

Novelty Minnow Float

This trolling-style minnow bucket was designed to be pulled behind a rowboat. It was made of "all metal galvanized iron in best-backed green enamel" with gold trim and silver lettering and decorations (made between the early 1900s and 1920). It was 24" long x 7 1/2" in diameter with a 10-quart capacity. (Terry McBurney photo)

$150-$800

Hartford Minnow Float

was made by the Shinners-Russell Co. of Hartford, Wis., circa early 1900s. It had a torpedo-shaped body designed to be trolled behind the angler's rowboat, with a bottom ballast to keep it "afloat, always right side up." The rear portion was perforated to aerate the minnows while the forward portion was a closed chamber protecting the minnows while being towed. It was 28" long x 7" in diameter, weighed 4 pounds, was made of "galvanized iron" and painted green. The original retail was $2.50. (Charles Arthur Collection)

$100-$300+

Trolling-style Minnow Pail

(manufacturer unknown) This unusual galvanized trolling bucket was originally painted an O.D. green, measured only 22" x 6" and weighed 4 1/2 pounds. It came with an outside bottom ballast that may have also acted as a rudder to keep it towing straight. It also has a unique storage compartment on top of the slide-open lid. You could store different bait, such as crawfish, in it or extra tackle or even your lunch. And it had a substantial grip-style carry handle on one end that was far sturdier than either the Novelty or the Hartford handles. (Charles Arthur Collection)

$500-$700

Lucas #28 Rectangular Floating Minnow Bucket

(Utica, N.Y.) This rare minnow bucket had a 10-quart capacity and came in a dark green japanned finish. It measured 11" high x 10 1/2" wide x 5" deep. There were two 1" holes on each end to allow air to circulate, and the lid was recessed so you could put ice on top to keep the water cool. A 1917 Abercrombie and Fitch catalog (the only catalog I have found it in) claimed that its shape was more convenient to carry, more compact thus taking up less room and it could be carried in a suitcase. Just don't spill any water! (Charles Arthur Collection)

$400+

Double-ended Boat-Style Minnow Bucket

(Manufacturer unknown) I found this unusual minnow bucket last summer at the Allegan, Mich., Antique Market and so far have not be able to identify it. Some collectors call this style "The Ark" and others call it the "double-ended boat-style." The triangular, pointed ends are flotation chambers, so this is a floating minnow bucket. This example was in rough, rusty condition and was worth only $40-$50. (Terry McBurney photo)

$150-$300 in good condition

Three Copper Minnow Buckets

A few minnow buckets were made out of copper. Most were made by individual blacksmiths or tinsmiths and were sold locally. The only "production" copper minnow buckets that I have found were the Halls telescopic buckets and a Shapleigh Hardware CM10 10-quart cold-rolled copper minnow bucket which is on the left. It retailed for $11 in 1935, a very expensive price considering this was in the depths of the Depression. The middle 11" oval copper bucket was locally made, and the oval bucket on the right (7" high x 14" x 8") is commonly called an "Indiana-style" bucket and was made by an Indianapolis-area craftsman named "Dye." Copper minnow buckets have a wide price range based on the condition as well as the quality and the styling. (Charles Arthur Collection)

$200-$1,000 each

Air-Fed Floating Minnow Bucket

*(Air-Fed Mfg. and Stamping Co., Quincy, Ill.)
The angler would pump up the air chamber with the attached brass pump that would then automatically feed a bubbling supply of air into the water, keeping the minnows fresh and lively. It was offered in two sizes, 8-quart and 10-quart, and was available during the 1920s through the 1930s. It had an interesting warning on the label: "The air chamber in this bucket has been tested to 25 lbs. Never pump it more than this amount of pressure. DO NOT FILL AT A FILLING STATION. Test pressure after eight strokes of the pump." It makes you wonder how many exploded? (Ken Irwin Collection, Terry McBurney photo)*

$50-$100

The Jones Aquarium Minnow Pail
TWO PAILS IN ONE

MINNOW CONTAINER

1—Valve
2—Towing Ring
3—Depth 2½ inches
4—Hollow Wire where air escapes
5—Minnow Trap

DESCRIPTION

The Jones Minnow Pail consists of an outer receptacle made of galvanized steel on inside of which is a galvanized wire inset or minnow container provided at its top with an oval air chamber and fitted with a valve to receive ordinary bicycle pump by means of which air is supplied into air tank. Small tube from air tank supplies constant stream of air bubbles at bottom for six hours. Air tank refilled in two minutes. Will keep minnows alive indefinitely as long as air supply is maintained. It has been thoroughly tested for several seasons. Common sense shape. A joy to the true sportsman. Inquire of your dealer or order direct. Each pail guaranteed. **THE DESHLER MAIL BOX CO., Deshler, O.**

No. 200—8 qts.—6x8x15
Price, complete, . . . $2.75

No. 300—12 qts.—6x10x15
Price, complete, . . . $3.00

"Jones" 8-quart Aquarium Minnow Pail Ad

from 1911. (courtesy of Larry Smith, Great Tackle Advertisements 1874-1955)

"Jones" 8-quart Aquarium Minnow Pail

was made by the Deschler Mail Box Co. of Deschler, Ohio, during the 1910s through the 1930s. It was a "race-track-shaped" oval bucket that contained an air chamber that you pumped up with a bicycle pump. It would force a stream of air bubbles through the water, aerating the minnows for four to six hours. The air chamber also kept the minnow pail afloat if the angler wished to use it in a lake or a stream. Examples have been found in dark green, red and black. (Don Stone Collection, Terry McBurney photo)

$175

"Jones" 12-quart Aquarium Minnow Pail

The main difference between the two sizes of Deschler's "Jones" Aquarium minnow pails was that the 12-quart version had a recessed outside lid that you could put ice on to keep the water cool. I have seen a 12-quart Jones Minnow Pail with a "Falls City Fish logo," so it would seem that either Deschler made them for Falls City starting in the late 1930s or that Falls City bought the rights to make them from Deschler. (Terry McBurney photo)

$175

Banta Aerating & Self-Cooling 10-Quart Oval Metal Minnow Pail

was popular over a long period of time from the early 1910s through the late 1930s. Almost all direct mail catalog retailers featured the Banta on their pages. It had all the features – sturdy galvanized construction that was covered with canvas. When the canvas was wetted, the water's natural evaporation would cool the contents. The angler was also instructed to push the internal hand pump every so often, which would freshen the water with little air bubbles. And there was a canvas wick that was attached to the top. This wick hung down inside the bucket and, like a lamp wick, it would draw water up to keep the canvas cover damp. All features were designed to keep the minnows lively and swimming. Very few Banta minnow pails have survived because the canvas material deteriorated from use. (courtesy of Larry Smith, Great Tackle Advertisements 1874-1955)

$150-$175

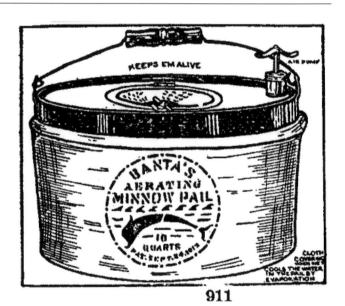

911

911 Banta Minnow Pail "Keeps 'em Alive". **Covered with cloth.** When wet and exposed to the sun's rays the evaporation cools the water in the pail. The air pump aerates the water. Cool water, well aerated, means live minnows. Pail is heavily galvanized inside and out, and will not rust. Oval in shape, with wood grip, bail handle, makes it easy to carry. Capacity 10 qts., each _____**$2.00**

Duplex Foldable Canvas Minnow Bucket

was "The best minnow bucket made–bar none!" according to the manufacturer, the Planet Company of Westfield, Mass. It also made other canvas products, including folding water pails, folding wash basins, folding creels, toiletry kits for men and feed buckets for horses. The Duplex came in two sizes, an 8-quart round version and a 10-quart oval model, and they were made out of a heavy-duty canvas material with rust proofed, spring steel parts. Circa mid-1910s through the late 1930s. (Jane Fladung Collection)

$50-$100

McConnell Minni-Sacs

(McConnell Mfg. Co., Cambridge, Ohio) were collapsible bait containers that came in three sizes : 1 1/2-quart, 3-quart and 8-quart. The lower half was made of canvas material and the upper half was mesh netting with a "duffel-style" drawstring. They were made during the 1940s. One 1941 ad states "Holds water for weeks. KEEPS BAIT ALIVE by diffusion of oxygen and evaporation thru sides and bottom...SETS UP LIKE A BUCKET – OR FOR WADERS – tie small sizes to belt. No more returning for bucket. WHEN tied to outside door handle of car, bait will stay alive on long trips!" (Terry McBurney photo)

$50 each

Allred "10-quart Special" Oval Minnow Bucket

(Indianapolis, Ind.) This is an early heavy-duty galvanized non-floating minnow bucket with a simple black stencil and a brazed-on oval company logo. It was probably made in the 1910s or early 1920s, and is by the only Indiana minnow bucket manufacturer that I have seen. (Terry McBurney photo)

$50-$100

Shakespeare #759 "Intrinsic" 10-quart Round Floating Minnow Bucket

(Kalamazoo, Mich.) Shakespeare started selling minnow buckets in about 1916 and carried an extensive lineup of nine different styles. I believe they were all made for Shakespeare by Cream City (Geuder, Pasachke & Frey Co., of Milwaukee, Wis.). There were three different sizes of "Intrinsic" minnow buckets, 8-quart, 10-quart and 12-quart, and each was made of tin-plated steel that was painted a dark green with gold striping. These are extremely rare early minnow buckets. (Randy Spagnoli Collection)

$100-$300

Shakespeare #7785 5-Gallon "Stay Alive" Minnow Bucket

(Kalamazoo, Mich.) The 5-gallon size of the Stay Alive minnow bucket (7 1/2" high x 17" in diameter and 12 pounds) was introduced in the mid-1930s primarily to transport small fish. To quote from the 1936 catalog, "...the squat 5-gal. size bucket designed originally for transporting goldfish, especially the "Giant" variety...fish are shipped in this bucket great distances by goldfish breeders without a change of water...." Shakespeare offered special prices to conservation departments and commercial hatcheries. In fact, this minnow bucket was marked with a stencil that read "Michigan Dept. of Conservation – Division of Fisheries – Hastings." (Bob Rogers Collection, Terry McBurney photo)

$100-$150

Falls City #110 "Winner" 10-quart Round Floating Minnow Bucket

First Version (Louisville, Ky.) "Falls City" was the brand name of Stratton Terstegge, a large Louisville hardware wholesaler. It manufactured minnow buckets, bait containers and tackle boxes under the "Falls City" name and sold them to sporting goods stores, direct mail catalog houses, sporting goods wholesalers and to other hardware wholesalers across the U.S. It was the largest minnow bucket manufacturer from late 1920s through the early 1970s, when plastics took over. There were two sizes of "Winner" buckets, 8-quart and 10-quart. The first versions of the "Winner" minnow buckets were made of tin-plated steel with a dark green japanned finish with gold bands and white lettering. These are extremely rare early minnow buckets. (Randy Spagnoli Collection)

$100-$300

Falls City #110 "Winner" 10-quart Round Floating Minnow Bucket

Second Version (Louisville, Ky.) This picture shows the second generation of the "Winner" minnow bucket. It was made out of a dark green painted tin-plated steel with the famous green and gold Falls City "fish" transfer. The "Winner" was still being made in the 1930s in two sizes: 8-quart and 10-quart. (Charles Arthur Collection)

$50-$75

Falls City #7634 "Expert" 12-quart Oval Floating Minnow Bucket

(Louisville, Ky.) This is an early Falls City heavy-duty galvanized floating minnow bucket with a simple black stencil, circa late 1920s. The stencil was later dropped and replaced by the famous Falls City green and gold "fish" transfer. After World War II, the logo was changed again and became the popular red or blue "Anglers Choice." There were two sizes of "Expert" oval minnow buckets, 10-quart and 12-quart. Value is based on condition and whether it is an earlier version. (Bob Rogers Collection, Terry McBurney photo)

$35-$100

Falls City #608 "Submarine" 8-quart Round Floating Minnow Bucket

(Louisville, Ky.) This unique style was a one-piece galvanized floater. The dome-shaped perforated top had an air chamber attached to the bottom side of the lid. The float allowed the bucket to ride just submerged under the water's surface and water would circulate through the perforated holes. This rare style was made in two sizes, 8-quart and 10-quart. It was relatively short-lived, being made for about five years in the early 1930s. Value is based on the condition of the bucket and the condition of the green and gold Falls City "fish" transfer. (Blane Bollaert Collection, Terry McBurney photo)

$75-$100

Three Sizes of Falls City Minnow Buckets

with their "Angler's Choice" logos. The "Angler's Choice" logo first appears as early as 1941 and lasts through the early 1970s. The photo shows the most popular model, the #7810 round 10-quart, galvanized two-piece floater; the #7824, which was an oval 12-quart, two-piece floater; and the #7830, which was a round 30-quart, two-piece floater, the largest minnow bucket. All of these styles came with a galvanized float chamber welded under the lid of the insert. Falls City introduced its "Dylite" foam float chamber in 1959, which was much less expensive to make but worked just as well as the welded chamber. There are a lot of Falls City "Anglers Choice" minnow buckets out there. Values are based on the condition of the bucket and the logo, and whether it's an early version. (Jane Fladung Collection)

$10-$60 each

Two "Hardware Company" Minnow Buckets

Shapleigh Hardware (St. Louis, Mo.) and Belknap Hardware (Louisville, Ky.) A Shapleigh "Diamond Brand" oval 10-quart, galvanized, two-piece floater from the mid-1930s and a Belknap Hardware "Blue Grass" round 10-quart, galvanized, two-piece floater. Shapleigh's "Diamond Brand" originally came from its well-known line of Diamond Brand knives. It also used this name on its top-end minnow buckets and other fishing tackle. Value is based on the model and the condition of the bucket, especially the logo. (Charles Arthur Collection)

$60-$125 each

Two great-looking logos

A "Kingfisher-branded" 10-quart, galvanized, floating minnow bucket sold by the Edward K. Tryon Co., a Philadelphia sporting goods wholesaler, and a Covey Minn-Safe 10-quart, galvanized, non-floating minnow bucket (Covey Mfg. Co., Holdenville, Okla.). Note the grooves on the lower half of the Covey bucket, which are unusual (circa late 1940s-1950s). (Jane Fladung Collection)

$35-$60 each

Four Round 10-quart, Two-Piece Floating Minnow Buckets

Falls City (Stratton Terstegge, Louisville, Ky.) made both the "Green River" and the "Minn-O-Lung" minnow buckets. The "#10F Green River" was available as a catalog item during the late 1940s. The "Minn-O-Lung" was available in the late 1930s. It featured an insert that had an inverted cone-shaped chamber at the bottom, designed to self-aerate the water. Air was captured inside this inverted cone when you lowered the liner into the bucket's outer shell that was filled with water. The air was slightly pressurized and was released as a stream of air bubbles through a tiny hole in the bottom of the insert. The "Sport King" bucket was Montgomery Ward's private label brand name, and the "Mohawk" bucket was made by Horrocks Ibbotson, a large manufacturer and distributor of tackle located in Utica, N.Y. (Grandville Island Sports Fishing Museum, Vancouver, B.C., John Keith-King photo)

$25-$60 each

Mit-Shel Stamping Mfg. Co.

(Quincy, Ill.) and Faris Co. (St. Louis, Mo.) Minnow Buckets. Mit-Shel was a major minnow bucket producer from the late 1930s through the 1940s, selling to wholesalers, larger retailers and catalog houses. Faris was a smaller manufacturer, and I have only identified a few styles of Faris minnow buckets. They were all well made and uniquely styled. The three pictured galvanized minnow buckets are a Mit-Shel "Leader" 10-quart, two-piece floater; a Mit-Shel Air-O-Matic 6-quart, "breather-style" minnow bucket with a cellulite liner; and a Faris "Lifetime Floater" 10-quart, two-piece floater. (Jane Fladung Collection)

$35-$60 each

Faris Feather Weight Floater Aluminum Minnow Bucket

(St. Louis, Mo.) This round 8-quart, two-piece floater with the unusual float built into the insert's lid was one of the most attractive designs ever made. Value for this relatively rare minnow bucket is based on condition and whether the original paper label survived. (Jane Fladung Collection)

$25-$50

Frabill "Fullflote" Round 10-quart, Two-Piece, Galvanized Floating Minnow Bucket

*(Milwaukee, Wis.) Frabill Manufacturing began business in 1946, making a fish stringer called the "6 in 1." Several years later, it started to produce minnow buckets in its Milwaukee plant. This early example was made in the late 1940s or early 1950s. There are a lot of Frabill buckets out there, so value ranges from $10 to $60 based on the condition of the bucket, the logo and the age of the model. Frabill is the only metal minnow bucket manufacturer still in business today. It currently markets an extensive lineup of landing nets, portable ice shelters, ice jigging rods, bait containers and bedding, plastic minnow buckets and, last but not least, a galvanized wading bucket and an 8-quart, galvanized minnow bucket (**www.frabill.com**). (Terry McBurney photo)*

$10-$60

Wading Buckets

Used by wading fishermen in streams, lakes or on saltwater flats, they held any kind of bait from minnows to worms and leaches to shrimp. These were worn over the shoulder using a canvas strap. The two Old Pal wading buckets (Lititz, Pa.) are made of galvanized steel. They show an early "Old Pal" logo and the later Old Pal/Woodstream logo. The third wading bucket was called "The Angler" and was made by Gemmer Engineering, Richmond, Ind. This aluminum wading bucket had a hinged masonite top and came with a cellulite liner. Copy on the top reads: "Worms and minnows keep active, they breathe through this bait container." (Jane Fladung Collection)

$15-$30 each

Two Early Galvanized Minnow Buckets

(Makers unknown circa 1920s) The one on the left was probably made by a small local manufacturer. It is 11 1/2" tall x 9 1/2" in diameter. The one on the right, probably hand made by a small-town tinsmith or farmer, measures 14 1/2" tall x 10 1/2" in diameter. (Terry McBurney photo)

$25-$40 each

Clipper Heated Ice Fisherman's Minnow Pail

by E.L. Walstedt & Co. (Minneapolis, Minn.) This was an uncommon minnow bucket found mostly in the northern ice fishing states. There was a 4 1/2"-high glass fuel jar with a wick fueled by kerosene or fuel oil. The ice fisherman would light it and then place it in the special compartment. As you were fishing, you could check to see if the lamp was still burning by looking through the side "view port," which was covered with a thick piece of clear plastic (there was no "view port" on first versions of the Clipper, the ones with the wooden covers). Then the inner bucket filled with minnows would be placed inside this outer shell and covered with the lid. The heat from the little fuel jar would keep the chamber warm and protected from the freezing outside temperatures. This kept the minnows lively and ready to catch bigger fish. The first version of the Clipper came with a wood lid that was soon replaced with metal ones. When you find the earlier wood-covered version, most of them have some fire damage. (Jane Fladung Collection)

$75+

Lucky Floater Minnow Bucket

by the Lucky Floater Company (Chicago, Ill.) This bright green 10 1/2" tall bucket had an unusual shape, with a narrow 7" diameter base section and a wider 9" diameter top section, which floated the bucket. Inside there was a spring-loaded rod that when you pulled upward to the right, the bottom cover plate opened. This allowed the angler to lower the water level or empty the bucket completely without tipping it over. There was a permanent perforated bottom cover that kept the minnows inside the bucket when the cover plate was opened. An upward pull on the rod handle with a turn to the left closed the cover plate. (Jane Fladung Collection)

$70+

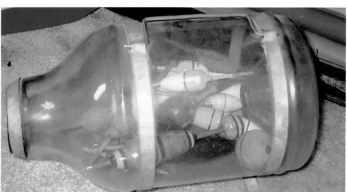

Small minnow trap

unmarked, about 11" long on metal legs connected by the metal straps around the trap. Rebel lures counter display is pre-ZIP and sells for about $100 with lures. A few collectible bobbers and floats are inside it in the second photo. I paid $200 for it in 2003; bobbers and floats vary from a few dollars to nearly $100 for some of the early ones with brass ends and roller mechanisms. The nicest one in this group is the cylindrical one with a ball bobber on top, about $50.

Minnow trap, $200+
Rebel unit, $100+
Bobbers, $5-$50 each

Common Orvis minnow trap

about 13" long. I sold one at a farm auction in 2002 for $125.

$100-$150

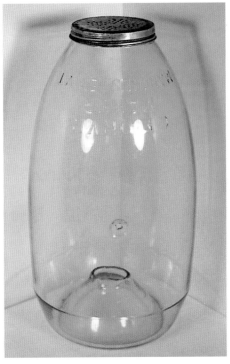

Bob-Bet bait boxes

The one on the right is the original Walter S. Cole model from Beaver, Wis. The one on the left is the Frabill model after buying the rights to it.

$15-$20 for Cole model; $10-$15 for other

Small minnow trap

with an interesting shape.

$200+

Old Pal bait box

nicely embossed.

$20+

Old Pal

very old bait box, with a Hendryx raised pillar reel.

Box, $35+; reel, $40-$60

Tackle Boxes

Most tackle boxes are not collectible, but many are of some value and a few are very collectible indeed. UMCO boxes are superior products and have gained a great collector following. Many of the early metal boxes made by Heddon, Shakespeare, Falls City, Kennedy and others also have value. Early boxes by Vom Hofe are very valuable. However, most of the tackle boxes from the 1960s and newer are merely anchors to the average collectors, weighing them down. One real problem with tackle box collecting is the shipping. Due to weight, it is very costly to ship a box. Another issue is room to display them: they are large and demand a lot of space. Of course, the ideal situation is to collect lures and reels, then fill the tackle boxes with the collection.

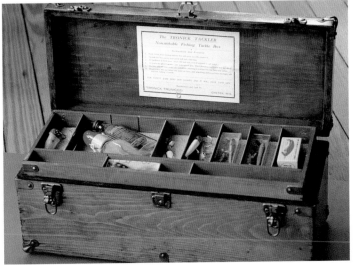

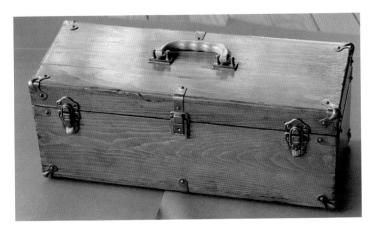

Tronick Tackler wooden tackle box

They simply do not come much nicer than this one. Note the reinforced corners and beautiful brass hardware everywhere. The box is full of Wisconsin lures, including some Worth and a couple of Musky Lunch lures, among many others. One recent sale exceeded $500.

$250+

Beautiful musky fishing box

made by Ron Kommer, Sandy Lake, Pa. He sold me this last year and all of the drawers are divided with a light brass material. Kommer sold me all of his lures and fishing equipment, including the items shown in Chapter 8. This box is large enough to sit upon while fishing.

$200+

Early Shakespeare tackle box

with japanned interior, as shown at the end of the Shakespeare Reel section in Chapter Two. This was my find of finds for tackle boxes due to its contents.

$50+

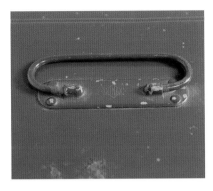

Early Climax tackle box

by Horrocks-Ibbotson. Outside is repainted, but the inside is original and it still has the nice decal.

$50+

Union Hardware tackle box

all original with key.

$75+

Photo essay

of a very early japanned tackle box with multiple layers, believed to be a Vom Hofe or Mills. Japanned black exterior with gold trim and letters of angler on box. Details of the box and some of the contents are shown. This is the box in which I found one Julius Vom Hofe reel and another unmarked hard rubber fly reel (shown in Chapter Two). This also had many early Archer baits and other items from the late 1800s and early 1900s. The fishing regulations are from 1947, which is likely when this one was "put away." Contents vary widely from a few dollars to maybe $50 for the "priest."

Box, $200+

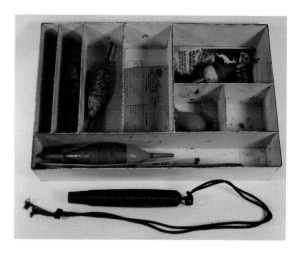

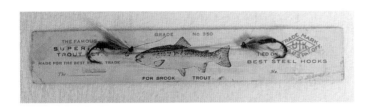

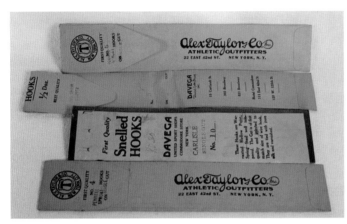

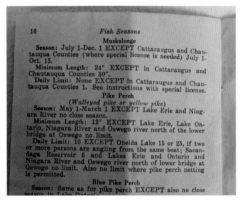

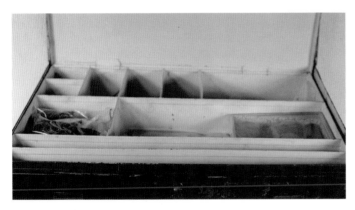

Heddon cantilever box

two tray. Some of the Shakespeare reels shown earlier in boxes came from this tackle box from a friend.

$50+

"Pocket Tackle Box"

non-descript. Not real valuable, but a cute little multi-compartment box ideal for fly-fishing with poppers.

$5

Saltwater box

made on the Pacific Coast, circa 1950s.

$75-$100

Large wooden tackle box

nicely made, unmarked, with lure tray and nice brass hardware, likely a "kit" box.

$150-$200

Small wooden tackle box

with brass corners and hardware. Box is only 9" long, 5" wide and 3" tall. It is shown as found with contents.

$75-$125

Chetek tackle box

from Chetek, Wis. These are very collectible boxes made by Chetek boat and tackle company. The wood has such a mellow tone from rubbing it with cranberry oils, a large cash crop in the Northwestern Wisconsin region.

$250-$350

Bi-color box

shallow aluminum, has plastic lure insert, about 4" deep. It is unmarked.

$10-$20

Ted Williams Model 34454

three-tray tackle box with brass hardware and the top tray has polyurethane foam for placing small lures and flies. This box is 14" x 7" x 7 1/2". This was made only for Sears.

$75+

Meadow Brook old metal tackle box

likely made by Union Hardware for Sears Roebuck & Co. Meadow Brook is another of the Sears trade names used for its earlier fishing items, as is J.C. Higgins shown in the reels chapter.

$50-$75

Kennedy tackle box

I still use. It's in rough shape so not worth much.

$10+

Kennedy box

hip roof aluminum with nice large compartments. This is a little different story than the steel boxes shown earlier. This box is very nice and makes a great storage spot for those collectible lures and reels.

$75+

Earlier Kennedy

with the signature scrollwork on top, leather handle, nice large compartments for large lures. One reason I like the Kennedy "Kits" is because one can store lures in them so well. Many of the boxes from the 1950s-70s were designed only for spinning or smaller casting lures. This is one problem with many UMCO boxes. But the Kennedy boxes are from an era of large lures that we all love to collect.

$20-$30

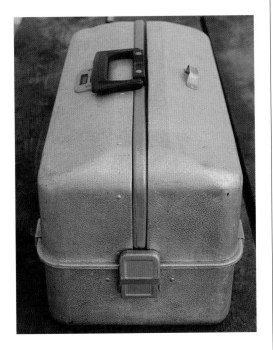

UMCO boxes

are the king of all aluminum boxes. This is a 1000A. They sell very well to collectors.

$75-$100

Model 173 A UMCO box

in aluminum. Note the reel holder in top.

$50-$75

Model 3500 U tackle box

by UMCO. This is the Umcolite line, made out of a light plastic material that is very strong. These are wonderful boxes and this one is in excellent shape.

$250+

Model 173 US box

designed specifically for spinning, in Umcolite material. Also, note the reel holder.

$100+

Old Pal box

on the left from the 1950s in metal. The one on the right is an early 1950s Plano box designed specifically for spinning, in the Plano marbleized plastic style. I have found a few of the nice casting-type boxes in this material, but this is the one and only spinning box I ever found.

$25 for Old Pal; $50+ for the neat early Plano

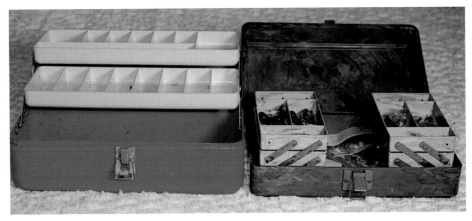

Early Falls City tackle box

(Louisville) with Japanned interior, showing one of the pull-out trays (there are three, one large and two small) and some related collectibles. The most unusual item is the Weber Hoochy feather duster, one-of-a-kind made by the factory and found in archives when purchased.

$75+

Chapter Five:
MORE

The number of chapters in this book could go on forever it seems, but we must end somewhere: my editor insists. In this final chapter are placed many other collectibles of interest and in demand today by the collector of angling items. It is not by any means complete, but should give one a good idea of most of the areas for which we have some idea of values. The chapter is broken down into sub-headings, each of which could be a separate chapter if I had more time and space available. I did not include boats and motors as originally intended, due to time and space constraints.

A float collection

that I own.

$2,000+

Wisconsin Guide badge

from 1917 issued to Tim Kennedy at the age of 20.

$200

Awards, Badges, Fobs

Many unusual collectibles exist that would fit into this miscellaneous category. Magazines such as *Field and Stream* gave awards for different fishing categories. One of the prizes was a nice metal award that has now become highly desired by collectors. They normally sell for at least $75 each and up to $200 for some types. There are also many watch fobs of interest, related to fishing tackle and fishing. Badges include items given away at conventions to the exhibitors, such as an Evinrude Motor badge. Many states used badges for conservation officers and also for licenses. The guide and conservation badges are in this section and the license badges will be covered in the next section. In addition to these items, some fishing lure, rod and reel companies also distributed items such as lapel pins, tie clasps and other jewelry advertising their products. Any of these small items are collectible, and many of them are rare and in high demand. Also, they often go unnoticed by collectors. They are often found in miscellaneous areas of antique stores and malls, and dealers do not always classify them as "fishing collectibles."

Variety of collectibles

with four badges top center from Beaver Falls Sportsman's Club (1969 and two 1977) and a Beaver County Conservation badge from 1969. Also shown are a variety of other collectibles including the tip of a 8" float, Zebco De-Liar, scale, Weber line, old disgorger, Mustad hook box and Mucilin dressing. The pliers at the bottom were made by Detty in the 1950s.

$10+ each

Wisconsin Guide License collection

from 1917-1942 for Melvin G. Long, Sr. Badges were issued each year except 1924, 1926 and 1928, when the previous year's badge was still valid. The 1917 "shield badge" is worth $200 and the other early 1918-1919 police type badges trade for $150. The round tintype badges trade for $50-$75 each.

$50-$200 each

Fishing Licenses

Fishing licenses have been a necessity for many decades in nearly every state and country where sport fishing is popular. The licenses themselves have taken on many forms and now are computer-generated ugly paper items in many states. However, historically many states prided themselves on the artwork involved with the licenses and those are indeed collectible. In Michigan, we were fortunate to have "fishing buttons" that also contained a paper license insert on the rear of the button (badge) for a few years in the late 1920s and early 1930s. Pennsylvania used this type of license for years, as did many other states. Overall, the most collector interest is in the button type of license.

All fishing licenses have collector appeal. Many seek out licenses from their birth year, their parents' birth years, some special year to them, or a series of years. The licenses are also interesting historical references and one can find quite a bit of information on some. Along with the license, each state issued some regulations for fishing and these too are collectible, sometimes of greater value than the licenses themselves (see the 1947 New York example in the Tackle Box section). In addition to licenses and fishing regulations, some states also issued "shipping permits" that needed to be included if any fish were shipped home from the out-of-state angler's catch. Finally, the other point of interest to collectors is "in-state" versus "out-of-state" licenses, with the out-of-state generally being harder to find and more valuable due to scarcity.

In addition to the licenses, many states have also issued special "stamps" for trout or some other species. Internet license sales have ruined the Trout Stamp collecting in Michigan, but for generations the Trout Stamp was the most beautiful aspect of one's license. As with duck stamps, the stamps produced by states for particular species are crossover collectibles, with both anglers and stamp collectors competing for the same resource. Stamps are usually graded as to both condition and if signed or not. Unsigned mint stamps are worth the most, unless one finds a stamp signed by a famous person, such as President Hoover. A few states also issued original and limited artwork related to the species stamps, and it too is collectible and valued highly. Finally, a number of companies produced general conservation stamps with fishing themes and the United States Postal Service also issued many commemorative stamps related to fishing. Any of these stamps or First Day Covers by the USPS would be nice additions to a fishing tackle collection.

Michigan 1930 Resident Trout Badge

The back had a place for the paper license to be folded and inserted. The presence of the paper license increases the value. Also note the crack in the celluloid covering, which detracts some from the value. Most of the Michigan hunting or fishing licenses from 1929-1933 sell for a minimum of $100 to more than $300 each.

$100+

Special Muskellunge License

for Oct. 31, 1985, from New York in top left, and a variety of metal and plastic New York state Muskellunge tags. Note that the license (pink paper) has the fish spelled Muskellunge, but the tags are either Muskie or Muskalonge.

$10-$20 each

1985 Wisconsin

Hook & Line Sturgeon tag, unused.

$10+

1996 Wisconsin

Hook & Line Sturgeon tag, unused.

$10+

Miscellaneous Paper Items

There are many paper items of interest related to fishing collectibles, in addition to the ones already mentioned. The first to come to mind is the highly valued and collectible area of catalogs. My book on Heddon catalogs covers that company's catalogs in detail and documents the value, often reaching three and four figures for early ones. The earliest catalogs would command five figures. This is true of many early (1900-1910) catalogs, and all of them are highly desired by collectors, both for reference and the intrinsic value of the catalog. The most valued catalogs seem to be from the major lure, and rod and reel makers. However, any manufacturer's catalogs are valuable.

In addition to the company catalogs, general wholesale house catalogs are also valued. These usually do not command the high dollar amounts of a specific catalog, such as a Heddon 1936, but are nonetheless invaluable as references. They often contain the only available color chart for some companies from a specific period of time.

Companies also produced fliers and special brochures to send to dealers to commemorate the release of a new lure, rod or reel. These little fliers are starting to gain collector interest and bring a few dollars each. Some very early ones will bring more than $100.

Posters and larger advertising items from any of the fishing tackle companies bring hundreds of dollars each, if original and in good condition. Many companies supplied large cardboard cutouts for store display and these are high demand items if one is ever lucky enough to locate one. A more common, but still highly valued find is the dealer display of lures.

Parts lists, repair directions, use directions and other items supplied by manufacturers are also collectible. This would include directions for using a collectible boat, motor, rod, reel or whatever is related to fishing.

Another category of collectibles is the area of fishing magazines and fishing annuals. Garcia published a wonderful annual, as did *Sports Afield*, and either of these items are valued. Any of the early magazines are also collectible, and the value simply increases as they get older. One caution is that they have to be in fine condition with no mildew or other odors, as this makes them about worthless.

Finally, books on fishing are an entirely separate category, but I shall include them here under general paper items. Many fine references exist on book collecting, but I shall include a few examples and values for the beginning collector of books on angling. Autographed books are always more valued by collectors and a special autograph will greatly increase a book's value.

Drewrys Beer Fisherman's booklet

This South Bend, Ind., brewery (in the hometown of South Bend Tackle) produced a nice little "give-away" booklet on fishing during the 1950s that is collectible, primarily a lake guide with a little information on tackle.

$10+

A colorful little booklet

from 1946 advertises the lines of Powerline Tackle Company of Grand Rapids, Mich. This is an unusual find in mint condition from a very small company. The booklet gives instructions for using the products and shows them.

$20+

Little Suzy display board

of lures from the mid-1950s from Charles M. Six Tackle Co. of Carthage, Mo. Hildebrandt of Indiana later offered very similar lures and so did Cotton Cordell lures. This board went back to Carthage to a collector who remembered the lures as a child.

$45

1929 catalog

from Guy H. Dixon & Son Co., Racine, Wis. This wonderful catalog not only has fishing and camping items, but also lists all fishing laws in America for 1929.

$75-$100

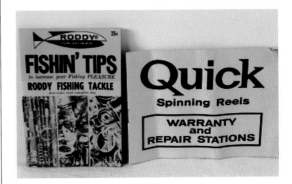

Roddy Fishing Tackle Engineers booklet

and Quick Reels booklet.

$5-$10 each

P & K 1947 catalog

and insert introducing the new Re-Treev-It fly reel by P & K.

$75+

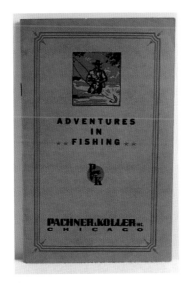

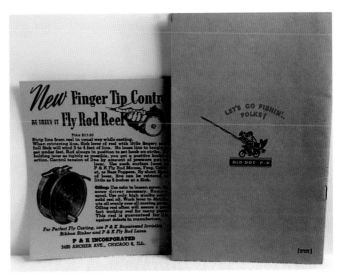

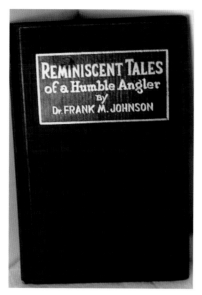

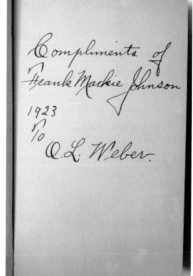

One-of-a-kind book

by Frank M. Johnson as it was signed and dated as a gift to O.L. Weber, founder of Weber of Stevens Point in 1923. The book is entitled Reminiscent Tales of a Humble Angler.

$500+, archival piece from Weber

Heddon catalogs

from 1978, 1981, 1982 and 1984. The 1984 catalog is the last one made, as the company designed it and printed it before selling to EBSCO, Inc. in 1983. All Heddon catalogs are valuable and some recent ones (such as the 1984) are very hard to find.

$50-$100 each, if mint

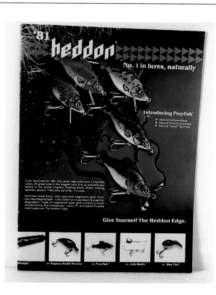

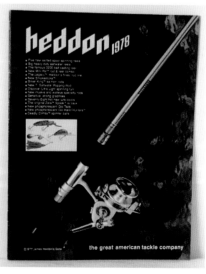

Nets, Gaffs, Blunts and Spears

As an attorney teaching police officers in Michigan, I always have fun on the legality of blunts, called "priests" in our state. It is illegal to carry a club with which to kill fish unless fishing, or if it is part of a collection being transported. It is easy to see why when one realizes how easily it will kill a pike or muskie. I do not find many of these tools in collecting, but once in a while an interesting blunt will come to fore that should be kept. I really do not think they have a lot of trade value yet, as most collectors do not even know they exist. However, some even have brand names on them and those would be valuable for certain.

Gaffs, on the other hand, are well known to collectors and many bring more than $100 each, especially the early Marbles and/or Nordlund brand gaffs. Gaffs were made with spring action, gripping action, snagging action, some folded, some extended, some were made by a local blacksmith. Again, there is not a "standardized" value on gaffs, but I think most are worth at least $10 and many are worth $100 or better.

There is some interest in collecting nets, especially the wooden framed trout nets. Ed Cummings from Flint, Mich., distributed a beautiful wooden framed net marked with his trademarked design that normally sells for $75 to collectors. There are other collectible nets available and all nets have interesting display functions for a lure collection.

Spears are an excellent fishing collectible to add to any collection as they go nicely with fish decoys in the north. They were also used for stream spearing in most of the country. Spears include both fish and frog spears, and major companies such as Pflueger made both, as did many local companies. Some collectors are only interested in collecting the "head" with the tines due to space constraints and others want the entire spear, handle and all. These are probably the most underrated of all fishing items at farm and estate auctions, often selling for $2-$5 each. A Pflueger spearhead alone is worth $50+, so one can see many bargains could be found in the field.

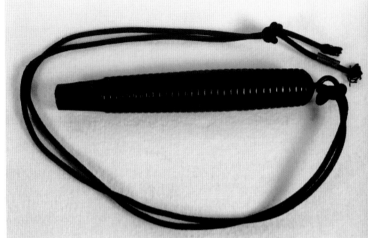

Hard rubber blunt

found in the old Japanned tackle box believed to be a Vom Hofe or Mills shown earlier.

$25-$50

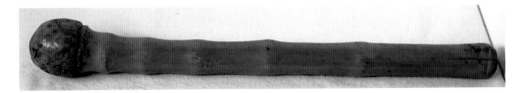

Very unusual heavy bamboo blunt

$25-$50

Grizzly brand gaff

new in the shipping carton, pre-ZIP code era, made by Maxwell Manufacturing, Vancouver, Wash.

$20+, shipping carton is worth about the same

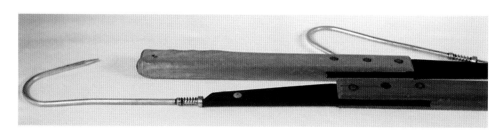

Unmarked folding gaffs

new, 1960s era.

$20+ each

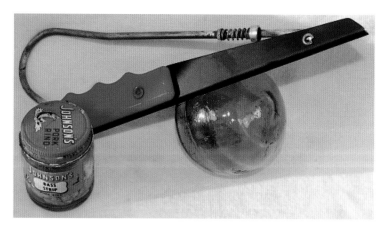

Unmarked folding gaff

shown with a Johnson Pork Rind bottle and nice old glass net float.

Gaff, $20; bottle, $10-$15; float, $25+

Two Finn-Lander gaffs

rare, made by Katchmore Bait Co. of Wisconsin.

$50+ each

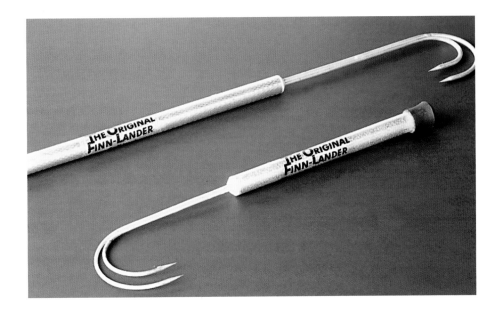

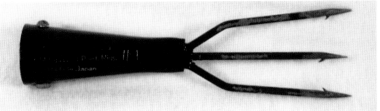

B & M Spears

B & M Co., West Point, Miss., Spear #1. This Japanese import dates from the mid-1950s and is in mint condition.

$25+

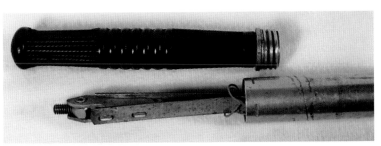

Unusual tube

contains a net and then becomes the net handle. It also has a screw thread in the end to allow another extension piece to be attached. This net was advertised in 1926 as the Chummy Getum Landing Net and sold new for $3.50.

$50+

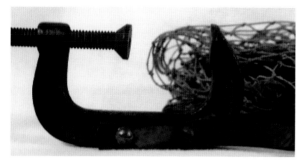

Interesting net

with vise handle for side of boat or dock.

$20

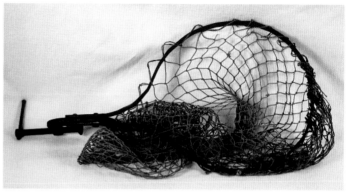

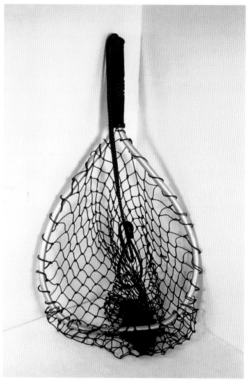

Aluminum nets

common in the 1950s-1960s that replaced the classic Cummings style wooden nets shown earlier in the book.

$5 each

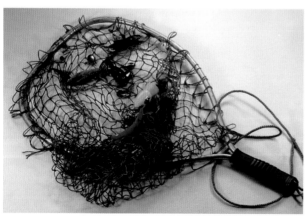

Miscellaneous Items

This section includes a sampling of the remainder of what I have noticed people collect related to fishing tackle. Items people collect include (at least): line spools, sinker boxes, hooks, hook displays, terminal tackle, sinker types such as trolley sinkers, salesman's samples, fish rulers, fish cleaners/scaling devices, knives, thermometers, oil cans, oilers, reel oil tubes/jars/bottles, mosquito repellants, catfish food tins, sardine tins, printer's blocks for advertising fishing items, glass and other floats, bobbers and wooden floats, and much more.

Off insect repellent bottle

from the 1960s-70s. This is quite recent, but makes a nice addition to the older ones shown later for a collection. This was a tackle box find, as are most insect repellents.

$5

Jitter-Bug insect repellent

from the 1940s. This is a great old bottle, especially for the Arbogast Jitterbug collector. Here we have a bug doing the "Jitter-Bug" to get away from the repellent. Made by Becker-Bischof Chemical Co. of St. Louis, Mo., one-ounce glass bottle with metal cap.

$40+

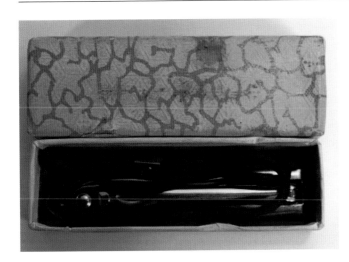

Angler's clips

in a two-piece cardboard box. A necessary item for every angler, especially the trout anglers along a stream changing flies.

$20+ in the box

Insect repellent

distributed by Skol Company, Inc. of New York, and made in Vermont. This is for mosquitoes, chiggers and other critters that are a nuisance to the angler. Likely 1940s or early 1950s, metal cap, nearly full, found in a tackle box.

$20+

Thomas Spinning Lures

dealer display card, still in the two-piece cardboard box used for shipping, all very clean. This nice item is from the mid-1960s and is an unusual find in the shipping box.

$50+

A neat early 1960s Rebel

fold-out display pack of a dozen lures.

$100+

Dealer display pack

Rebel (Plastics Research & Development Corp.) mid-1960s, for a dozen Gold Rebel/Shad lures with some others added. All lures were new in packages with paper inserts. I have sold a couple of these from $35 with seven lures to nearly $100 for a complete dozen.

$100 complete

Aero 1/0 Colorado Spinners

new on cards in the box. This dozen was full when found and some have been sold. Items such as this are valuable only if mint and extra clean. Collectors are not really interested in beat up or dirty cards, unless very rare. Individual carded lures have sold for $5-$10 each; complete dozen in box would be worth $50+ as a unit.

$50+; $5-$10 for individual lures

Nice selection of plastic and wooden bobbers

including three Mermaid bobbers and two Dolly Bobbers on the tubes. The striped cylindrical bobber at top left is a Heddon Winona bobber made of celluloid and found in most Heddon catalogs. Mermaids and Dollies $25+ each, Heddon: $10-$15, others from $5 to up to $100 for nice two-part wooden one with green bottom and red ball bobber on its top.

$5-$100 each

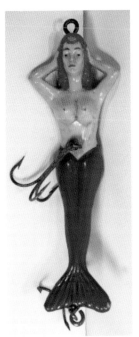

Mermaid fishing lure

$50+

Heddon "Whis-purr" spinning lures

display card with fold-out stand on back, Model 420 GFY-DC. This lure from the 1950s-60s is fairly non-descript, but found on a dealer card it is special. This one has five lures missing (sold).

$75+

Colorful Hump Tiger key chain fobs

(Hump Lures, Texas). These lures were made in the early 1980s when the last owners of Bingo Lures also owned Hump. They are very rare and were loaned to me by the former company owners, Ray and Patty Zapalac. Archive pieces.

$50+ each

Line box and spool

western brand Supertwist Cuttyhunk, 1950s.

$30+

Cisco Kid line

very rare, in the box, courtesy of Eason Mitchell.

$50+

Wooden line spool

for Gudebrod Gudeline with elephant symbol, front and back. Gudebrod Bros. Silk Co., Inc. was a major line company dating back to 1870, eventually also distributing some great lures in the 1960s-70s.

$20+ for nearly any wooden line spool with both labels in great shape

Bait-Life Live Bait Protector

new in two-piece cardboard box, made by Mackenzie Tool & Engineering Co., 86 Andrew Street, Springfield, Mass. This is pre-ZIP code, likely late 1950s. My friend Tony Zazweta found a gross (144) of these new in the original shipping box and I have sold many of them. All are new in the box with original paper inserts.

$15-$35 each

Shakespeare reel oiler

Similar to one also distributed by Orvis and others, this one has the famous reel company name on its front.

$20-$30

Two nice patches

advertising Storm Lures from the 1970s-80s. The black one was the last patch prior to the company's sale to Normark.

$5-$10 each

Pork rind jar

from American Fork & Hoe Co., a very unusual find. Al Foss lures depended on the addition of the pork rind for the wiggle and this early jar is not found often.

$20+

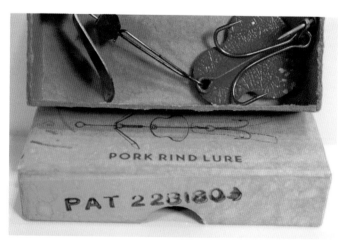

Donnie Wobbler

another unusual pork rind find, new in the box. This is a lure, but it shows the type of lure using pork rinds for fishing. It is rare, especially boxed as this one.

$40+

U-Fibb-R scale

and measuring tape. Many collectors know the De-Liar scale and tape, but have not seen the U-Fibb-R model. This one also has a small first aid kit and serves as a match-safe too. Note the little fish design under the name. This is the only one I have ever found.

$50+ boxed

Double-Duty fish pole holder

used, but with the box. The box is the hard thing to find. Many similar pole holders show up in tackle boxes from time to time.

$25 only if in the box

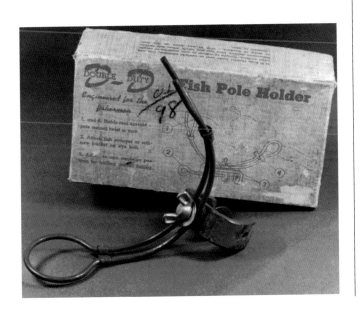

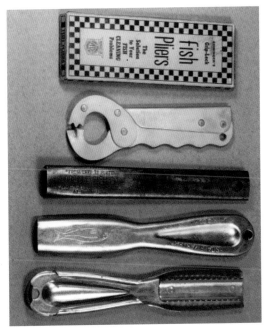

Fish pliers

and scalers, a variety from Wisconsin.

$10-$20 each

Rottler ice fishing rod/reel

from Wisconsin. Simple stamped reel similar to many shown in Chapter Two, wooden painted knob, simple sliding reel seat.

$50+

Blackstone Japan silk line

on a wooden spool in the original shipping box.

$70+

Wisconsin collectibles

Note the Rottler Ice Rod on left, the Finn-Lander gaff in back, the two box styles for Bob-Er-Lites, the Shinners minnow trap, some other minnow buckets, the Guncaster outfit that shoots your lure for you, the Musky tackle box and some decoys.

$25 each to nearly $1,000 for the Shinners

OK ice cleats

adjustable.

$20+

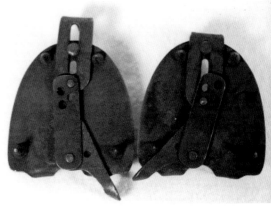

AR-BE reel brake

new in the box with papers, made by Koser Mfg. Co. of Wisconsin.

$35-$50 in box

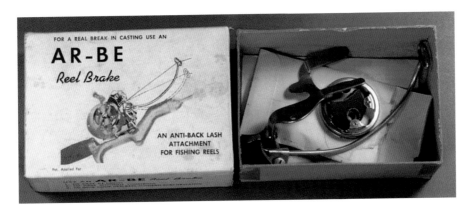

Oiler collection

owned by the author. Note also the neat little screwdrivers for reel repair.

$20-$40 each for most, a couple up to $100

Retriev-a Buoy

box and papers, made by Panef Mfg. Co. of Wisconsin. Another contraption to recover drowned equipment. Anglers will buy anything!

$35-$50 in either box type

Bob-Er-Lite boxes

and a couple of the lighting bobbers by the Pasch Brothers of Milwaukee, Wis.

$50-$75 boxed, $15-$25 without boxes

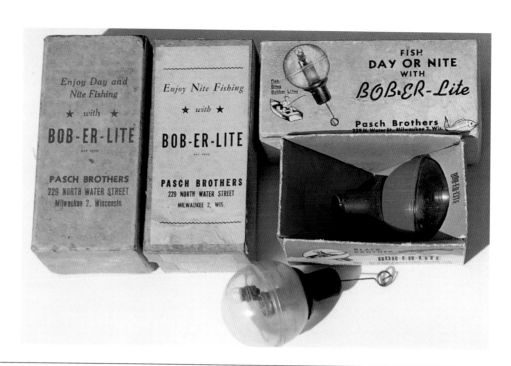

A variety of collectibles

purchased from Ron Kommer in 2003, including a small aluminum fly box, line spools, including a Garcia, snelled hooks, plastic line spool holder/tackle box, Mustad hooks in cardboard box, early Langley De-Liars and the Zebco version of the same, line preserver in boxes and a Mucilin tin, brass scales, metal de-gorger and an early pair of fish pliers (Detty Fish Gripper), a big white float, some early hooks, a Martin fly reel new in the box and some of the badges shown earlier. A close-up shows three De-Liars. The earliest one is the small one on the left next to a Pflueger Dry-Fly bottle with a bulldog trademark. There is also a 3-day fishing stamp for New Hampshire under the black Langley De-Liar.

$5-$50 each for most

Weber Tynex spinning line

store display piece, circa early to mid-1950s. It is covered with some of my favorite lures: Fin-Dingos, Flutter Fins, Punkinseeds, Dolls and others. Lures vary from lower end Optics at $20-$40, to Fin-Dingos and Punkinseeds at more than $100.

$200 for stand; lures $20-$100 each

Johnson Motors

and some Weber and Frost advertising plates.

$50-$200 each

Early Bowers lighter

in brass from Kalamazoo, Mich., and a Made in Hong Kong match safe modeled after Marbles types. Smoke 'em if you've got 'em!

**$75-$100 for lighter;
$25 for match safe**

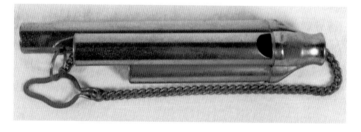

Surf rod holder

in tooled leather, California origin.

$25+

German-made silver boat whistle

$150+

Fish-Master

*stainless steel knife/
scaling combination.*

$40+

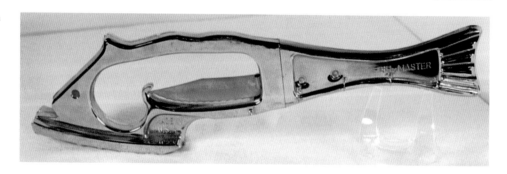

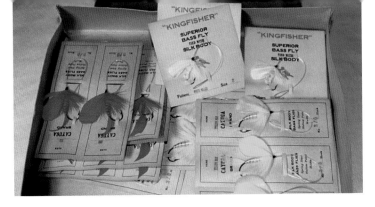

Rare flies

found in the Weber archives. The Kingfisher is the Tryon brand and I sold a few for $50+. All of the silk body flies sell very well and are very old. These had been stored with moth protection.

$20-$60 each

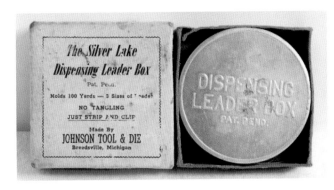

Silver Lake dispensing leader box

in Pat. Pend. box, made by Johnson Tool & Die, Breedsville, Mich.

$25+ boxed

Hook holders

in the shape of arrowheads. These, and hundreds of other styles, make a wonderful display of hooks, snelled and otherwise.

$10 each

Dealer display boxes

of Heddon River Runts and Deep 6 lures, along with a Pflueger Progress 1774 reel and two other Pflueger items. It is very unusual to find large lead weights like this marked. Heddon River Runt dealer dozens have sold for $1,000 twice this past year; the fly box is worth $40-$50, the sinker about $20 and the reel $30-$40.

$1,000 for dealer dozen

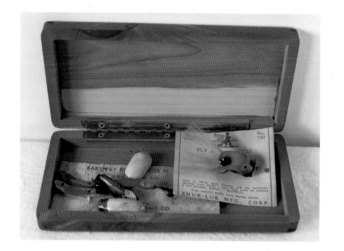

Fly box

from Don Gapen, Lapeer, Mich., a prototype with magnetic strips and a production version without them (he made both types). I have sold many for $50+.

$50+

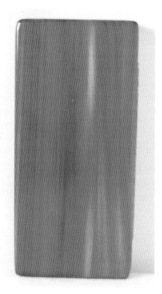 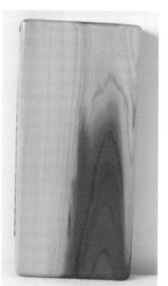 

Fly box

double top by Weber of Stevens Point with flies.

$75+

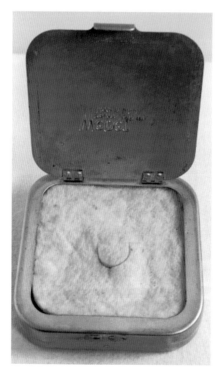 

Sinker tins

by Ideal (very common) and Lead Products (uncommon). Sinker tins sell for $5 to more than $100 depending on shape, maker, rarity, color and many other factors.

$5-$100 each

Unusual find

cardboard "Eze-Ty Hook Paks" from Grand Rapids, Mich.

$10

Dressing tins and kits

by Weber, Newton's and L & C.

Tins, $20 each; Weber in rare cobweb box, $50-$75

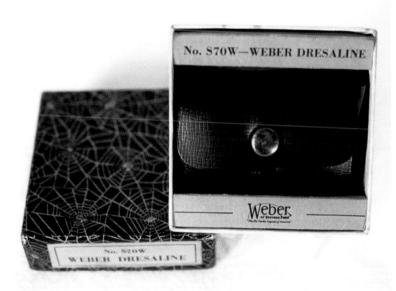

Line cleaners

grease tubes, oilers and varnish examples. The Penn tube in a double box is uncommon.

$10-$30+ each

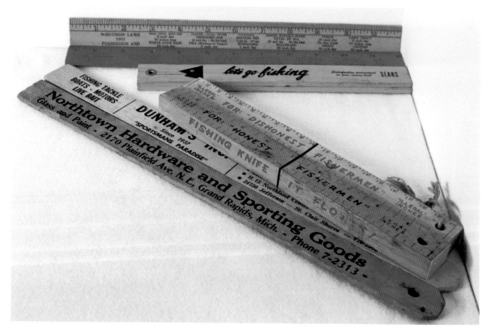

Collectible rulers

with the state fish laws on them. Also, note the Honest/Dishonest Fisherman Ruler/Knife combination.

$10-$25 each

Herter's Rod Repair Kit

new in the box.

$50+

Firelacquer kit

from Weber of Stevens Point on a 1963 Michigan Fish Laws ruler. The lacquer is actually from Weber Tackle.

$40+

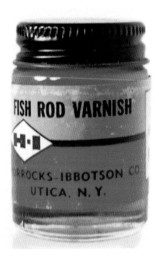

Horrocks-Ibbotson fish rod varnish

new from dealer dozen.

$20-$30 each

Hardy Bros Ltd. line dryer

Alnwick, England, with South Bend 1200 reel.

Dryer, $200+; reel, $35-$50

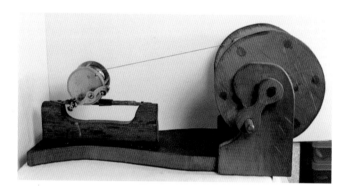

Interesting line dryer

folk made. Fish body platform with reel seat mounted on upright board and a large wooden spool to hold the line with wooden crank knob. Line is spooled off a Portage (Pflueger brand) Medina reel.

Dryer, $100+; reel, $25-$40

Heddon fish decoys

Books have been written on Heddon (I have done two) and also on decoys (Art Kimball's series is wonderful), but I had to at least include a couple of examples. Decoy on the left is the rare Heddon Batwing in Rainbow with a metal tail (earlier examples had wooden tail) and the one on the right is in Perch and is called a Four-Point by collectors. Both of these early 1900 examples are in demand. Batwings sell for the most, with $2,000-$4,000 being common.

$700-$4,000 each

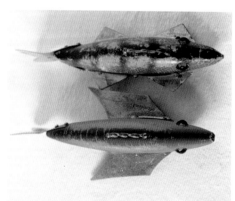

Bobbers and Floats

Lang's spring 2004 auction featured a salesman's sample case of 58 different floats from Pequea Tackle of Pennsylvania that was projected to sell for thousands of dollars. It did. Many of the floats in my collection shown later are Pequea. Some are Ideal. Many are unknown with any certainty, as many companies jobbed floats and bobbers. It is unusual to even find newer (1950s-1960s) bobbers new with packaging, as they were normally sold loose in tackle shops. A recent find was a Montague float from the classic era in its package and I did not hesitate to spend $150 for it. Recent bobbers only command a fraction of that unless they light, sing, reel in your fish or any number of ideas newer floats have shown. The Bob-Er-Lite showed earlier is one good example. Magic Float is another. Any float with identification is a plus, as we are really lacking in good data on this colorful and interesting fishing collectible.

Early floats are hard to date, as the painting style changed little on them over the years until modern times. However, some of the earliest have brass hardware on each end of the float. Another way to tell is the paint. Early ones all had lead-based paint and it is far more vivid than paints of the 1950s-1960s. Bobbers have come in a number of styles for years: cylindrical, oval, egg shaped, round, tapered round, quill style and long cylindrical with a round bobber added at the top. Many companies (Pequea and Ideal included) offered a simple bobber/float combined with a hand line wrapped around a little wooden frame (later plastic) that could then be transferred to the trusty cane pole or used as is for fishing. This was my standard fare as a small child when I went to the bait shop: new line and bobber on a winder for my pole. I sold a dealer dozen of these last year for more than $200 at a farm auction. I also sold an earlier version similar to the one shown in Lang's spring 2004 catalog for $500 nearly 10 years ago.

One of the impossible things about bobbers and floats is to identify the pure "cork" floats and bobbers without finding them in a display or package. They all are made of natural cork and thus look alike. It may be that we will come up with a technique to assist us in figuring this out, but I cannot see it in the near future (DNA analysis of the cork source is a little pricey for a bobber). But the patina of an old cork float is obvious and something that adds nicely to a fishing collection. Is there a more obvious symbol of peace and tranquility related to old fishing memories than a cork float at the end of a cane pole?

Old cork floats/ bobbers

$2-$5 each

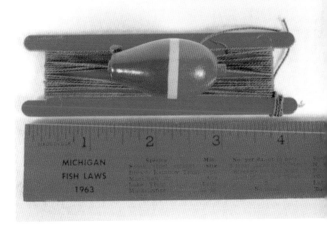

Ideal hand line

for cane pole usage, circa 1950s-60s. Wooden bobber with braided line on a plastic winder. This is similar to the set of 12 I sold for more than $200 last year.

$20-$25

Barracuda brand

(Florida Fishing Tackle) balsa float with paperwork. This 1950s float is a very common design, but rare to find with paperwork identifying the source.

$20-$25

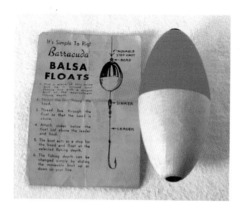
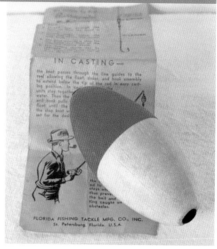

Similar float

with a bead that goes between the float and the stop taped onto the float. This is not marked, but is also from the 1950s and could be one of any number of companies' floats.

$10-$15

Arnold Tackle Speed Slip float

new on the card. This is from the late 1950s and was an unusual tackle shop find in the Upper Peninsula of Michigan five years ago at the Lake Ruth Marina. The owner had a few old items around that he boxed up and sold to me. This was one of them. It would be of little value by itself, but at least on its card it gives us one idea of what this 1950s tackle manufacturer was selling. Dylite is the trade name for the material used to make the float that was used first by Weber of Stevens Point. This, and the fact that Arnold sold out to Paw Paw in 1960, dates this squarely in the 1950s. Dylite was not used by most companies making tackle until about 1955.

$10-$20

Advertising bobber

for Doodle Oil. I have no idea of what Doodle Oil is, but it "Catches More Fish" because this bobber says so! It may be a catfish scent, but that is a guess. Bobbers, as lures, have been used to advertise all types of products and these novelty bobbers make an interesting addition to a collection.

$5-$10

Photo essay

of part of my float collection. This has some Pequea, Ideal, Heddon, Heddon copies, Japanese, folk made, varnished natural cork, 1950s-1960s common bobbers, and many more floats and bobbers. This little tour gives one a good sense of why we collect floats and bobbers. They are so colorful and beautiful. Many folks come and see my collection, and even those not interested in lures comment about the beauty of the floats.

$2,000+

Line Spools

Though a couple of line spools were shown earlier, we need to concentrate on this nice collectible a little more. Wooden line spools were a true work of art and advertising genius by early makers of line and tackle. The companies put a lot of effort into layout and design on the small circular labels glued onto the wooden line spools. There were a number of line makers, but Cortland, Gladding, Hall, Newton, Sunset Line & Twine, and U.S. Line Co. quickly come to mind as some of the big ones. Most of these companies furnished the lines for all of the big tackle makers as well.

I own most of the early paperwork for Hall from the 1800s and early 1900s, and have been researching the relationships with other companies. I can document many interesting connections, including relationships with Montague Rod Works, Shapleigh Hardware and Horrocks-Ibbotson.

Hall was a maker of bamboo rods and fishing lines. It sold these items under its own name and provided for many of the major wholesalers in the United States in the late 19th and early 20th centuries. I purchased a Hall salesman's sample of lines available in 1940, including a mint 1940 catalog. This gives one a good example to see all of the products being made under different names.

Value on line spools is determined by two different factors (in addition to condition, of course): colorfulness of the graphics and company affiliation. Wooden spools command more than most plastic ones, but some rare plastic line spools, such as the Wallsten (Cisco Kid) or some Heddon spools, still are valuable indeed. The major factor really is the graphics, but a "big six" line spool will usually have "added value" for an item. Condition must be very clean and it is ideal if the little center hole has not been punched out in the spool center, damaging the graphics. These are similar to floats/bobbers inasmuch as they are attractive even to those that do not collect fishing collectibles. This in turn drives the prices up a little due to competition for ownership with other collectors. Most wooden line spools start at $10 if excellent and some quickly go up to $50. The Japanese Silk example shown earlier in this chapter sold for nearly $70 with its cardboard shipping box. However, many fine examples can be purchased at shows and online for $10-$20 each and often even less. Two Winchester spools, both with center holes punched, sold for $100-$300+, so there is value in some of them.

Newton's Finger Lakes spool

for silk line.

$20+

Newton's Princess Pat spool

for braided linen line.

$20+

U.S. Line Co. Black Knight

brand early nylon spool and line.

$30+

Sunset Marina Cuttyhunk spool

and line for saltwater fishing.

$30+

Newton's Dictator 20-pound silk line

on wooden spool with great rooster.

$50+ if excellent, $20-$30 as is

Cortland Cam-O-Flage

Bait Casting line new on spool. This was a standard line in the late 1950s and early 1960s.

$10-$20

Jones Line Co. Kilrush Cuttyhunk wooden spool

$30+ if excellent, $10-$20 as is

Cortland "333" fly line

new in the box with papers. The small Cortland "333" line dressing tin, shown earlier in this chapter with the grease tubes, fit into the center of the spool and was shipped with the line.

$75+

Horrocks-Ibbotson "Imperial Special" fly line box

$40+, more than $100 if line was present

Western Auto "Silver Anniversary Nylon" fly line

new in the box, in container and line wiping cloth. This is a rare find from Western Auto and is in excellent shape, with only minor corner damage to the cardboard box. It is a recent find from a California 1950s estate.

$125+

Gladding's Comorant Cuttyhunk

on huge wooden spool new in the original two-piece cardboard box. This rare find also came from the Californian estate mentioned previously. This is a rare find with decal on the box, spool and line mint, and box in excellent condition.

$250+

Shakespeare Wexford Wonder Line

This was seen advertised earlier on Shakespeare boxes. It is fairly common compared to South Bend or Heddon spools, but still is a nice addition to a reel collection.

$10-$20 each without cardboard box, much more boxed

Heddon Monofilament spinning line

new on spool.

$20+

South Bend Strong-Oreno casting line

$30+

Photo essay

of Hall's 1940 lines in a salesman's kit, also showing mailing label and mint 1940 catalog. This was the 100th anniversary of the Hall Line Corporation. Note many of the different companies and brands used by Hall: "Badger" for Diamond Mfg. Co. of St. Louis; "Oh Boy" for Cohantic Line Co., Philadelphia; "Belknap" for the famous supplier of hardware and tackle from Louisville, and many others. This display has 23 wooden spools, five carded lines and five rolled lines. Some of these displays have been listed online but not sold, as the reserve was higher than the highest bid of $200. They are worth at least twice that much. The 23 wooden spools alone are worth $460 if broken up and sold individually as they are all mint and full (the Captain spool has the label off but it merely slid down). Apparently, someone found a few in an estate, but I have not seen any more recently. I bought mine privately about five years ago.

$600 minimum for entire collection, not counting $200 for the catalog

CHAPTER FIVE
More

EXPLORE THESE ADDITIONAL SPORTING COLLECTIBLES RESOURCES

Classic Fishing Lures
Identification and Price Guide
by Russell E. Lewis

Color photos and comprehensive identification and pricing information for 2,000 lures from Heddon, South Bend, Paw Paw, Pflueger, Creek Chub and Shakespeare, make this book the most comprehensive available! Includes company histories for each manufacturer.

Softcover • 8-1/4 x 10-7/8 • 368 pages
2,000 color photos
Item# CFL · $27.99

Classic Hunting Collectibles
Identification & Price Guide
by Hal Boggess

1,000 color photos of hunting-related items from the late 1800s to early 1940s including posters, calendars, pin backs, catalogs, shot shell boxes from Winchester, Peters Cartridge Co., Dupont, and others are featured with current collector pricing.

Softcover • 8-1/4 x 10-7/8 • 256 pages
1,000 b&w photos
Item# CHNT · $24.99

Tying Trout Flies
by C. Boyd Pfeiffer

Trout anglers can easily learn to make 100 popular and effective trout flies with these well-illustrated fly-tying procedures. Includes patterns for dry flies, wet flies, nymphs, and streamers, plus materials lists and step-by-step instructions from an expert angler.

Softcover W/Concealed Spiral • 8-1/4 x 10-7/8
160 pages • 150 color photos
Item# TYTF · $24.95

Old Fishing Lures & Tackle
6th Edition
by Carl F. Luckey with Clyde Harbin, Sr., "The Bassman"

The bible of lure collecting now features more than 3,000 collectible wooden and plastic lures and tackle with updated prices Extensive coverage is given to more than 200 collectible reels.

Softcover • 8-1/2 x 11 • 768 pages
2,400+ b&w photos • 64-page color section
Item# OFL6 · $34.95

Top Seller!

Warman's® Fishing Lures Field Guide
Values and Identification
by Carl F. Luckey & Clyde Harbin Sr.

This portable guide features detailed descriptions, sizes, colors, and up-to-date prices of nearly 1,000 old fishing lures from top lure manufacturers. Perfect for collectors on the go!

Softcover • 4-3/16 x 5-3/16 • 512 pages
1,000 b&w photos
Item# FLFG1 · $12.99

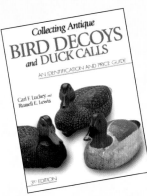

Collecting Antique Bird Decoys and Duck Calls
An Identification and Price Guide
3rd Edition
by Carl F. Luckey and Russell E. Lewis

Provides history and current pricing of the prominent duck and goose hunting decoy used over the past century-plus, and offers tips on identifying antique decoys-forgeries and fakes, techniques for restoration and repairs, and more.

Softcover • 8-1/2 x 11 • 496 pages
432 b&w photos • 64-page color section
Item# CABD3 · $27.99

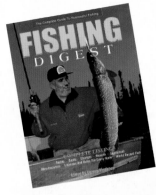

Fishing Digest
Edited by Dennis Thornton

Offers complete coverage of new fishing gear, tackle, and equipment, a directory of more than 1,400 leading fishing guides and charters, and state license fees and regulations. Lists top fishing resorts, state and national parks, and tourism resources by state.

Softcover • 8-1/2 x 11 • 352 pages
200 b&w photos
Item# FSH1 · $24.95

Heddon Catalogs Over 50 Years of Great Fishing 1902-1953
by Clyde A. Harbin, Sr. "The Bassman" and Russell E. Lewis

This updated volume of the world's most collectible fishing lures covers the famous Heddon catalogs from 1902-1953, and timeless articles on fishing techniques and hundreds of full-color photos.

Softcover • 8-1/4 x 10-7/8 • 256 pages
150+ color photos
Item# HDLTC · $24.99

To order call 800-258-0929 & mention offer ACB5

KP Books ACB5
700 East State Street, Iola WI 54990
www.krausebooks.com

When ordering direct, please include $4.00 for the first book and $2.25 each additional book to cover shipping and handling to US addresses. Non-US addresses please add $20.95 for the first book and $5.95 for each additional.

Residents of CA, IA, IL, KS, NJ, PA, SD, TN, VA, WI please add sales tax.